4 JUCOS

ALSO BY THE AUTHORS

Gridiron Gold

Y'all vs. US

Bull Cyclone Sullivan

Gridiron Glory

JUCOS

THE TOUGHEST FOOTBALL LEAGUE IN AMERICA

By:

X.M. Frascogna, Jr.
X.M. Frascogna, III
Martin Frank Frascogna

A Mississippi Sports Council
Publication

Mississippi Jucos, The Toughest Football League in America
Copyright 2011 by JUCO, LLC
All right Reserved.

Published by the Mississippi Sports Council,
a division of Velocity Sports and Entertainment, Inc.
Post Office Box 16067, Jackson, Mississippi 39236

Dust Cover design by Stadium Wrap, LLC.
Photographs and text layout design by Greg Pevey.
Unless indicated otherwise all photographs are the property
of the contributing school.

ISBN: 978-0-9789438-5-1
Printed in the United States of America

First Edition

In memory of
Brenda Marsalis

CONTENTS

///

JUCOS

FOREWORD

//

Mississippi's junior/community college system began in the 1920s, when the State Legislature approved agricultural high schools adding a thirteenth and fourteenth grade. The typical junior college in those days was a boarding school, still with a concentration on agricultural studies. Most of the students grew up working hard in tough environments--helping make crops or cutting timber on their family farms or taking odd jobs if they lived in town. These raw-boned farm boys were naturally drawn to the rough and tumble sport of football. Almost as soon as the first classes began, these young men, some of whom had never seen a game before, began playing football among themselves.

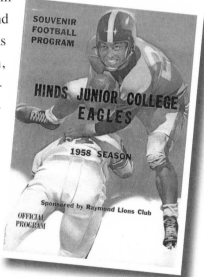

They soon mastered the basics and grew tired of playing against each other. So they sent an invitation--probably more like a challenge--to the boys from the junior college a few counties over. The winners of the first game would seek out yet another opponent to test their prowess, while the losers were honor bound to avenge their loss through a rematch. Soon these matches became more frequent and this led to the need for schedules. Schedules led to fixed seasons, which in turn led to the naming of champions. Football fever took hold and has never let up. The result is Mississippi's current system of junior/community college football.

Since those early days, many thousands of Mississippi men have played "Juco" football, to help them pay for college and to continue to pursue their passion for the sport beyond high school. For some of these boys Juco football was their best, or maybe only, chance at a better life. Perhaps they didn't have the money, or the grades, or the social maturity to go from high school directly to a university. Others perhaps, at age 18, were not quite big, or fast, or strong, or skilled enough to play football at a four-year college. But none of those obstacles prevented them from suiting up for the local Juco squad. Add their lifelong love of sports and the outdoors, and it is no surprise that Mississippi has provided a fertile soil for what has often been called the best junior college football in the nation.

As is so often the case in the football-crazy south, the gridiron is a major focus of campus life at Mississippi's community colleges. Football instills loyalty to the colleges in its students, alumni and the local communities, and brings thousands of people to campuses each fall. The game provides a stage on which country boys and small-time lads can excel by national competition in front of large audiences.

The quality of Mississippi Juco football is legendary. It is not surprising that in each of the two years prior to the publication of this book, a Mississippi Juco football alumnus was crucial in deciding the NCAA Division 1 National Champion. Terrance Cody of Mississippi Gulf Coast Community College was a member of the Crimson Tide team when the University of Alabama defeated Texas for the national title in 2010. This year, Nick Fairley of Copiah-Lincoln Community College was a War Eagle when his Auburn University team defeated the University of Oregon Ducks to claim the 2011 national championship.

For nearly a century, Mississippi has taken great pride in its Juco football, and the folks in the Magnolia State look forward to the gridiron battles on our campuses for generations yet to come.

Dr. Eric Clark

Executive Director

Mississippi Community College Board

Chapter
1

//

THE LEAGUE

One of the oldest and most colorful football leagues in America is tucked away in the deep south in a state that many consider the most football rabid place of all--Mississippi.

Way down south in the heart of Dixie you will find a self-contained, highly unique football ecosystem. The League consists of fourteen junior colleges that play what some refer to as renegade ball, while others describe it as innovative. Regardless of one's opinion, Mississippi Juco football is unlike anything else in the country.

Hidden from the national media the Juco teams in the Magnolia State compete for the League's highly coveted championship each year. Every game played during the season is a rivalry; each game matters. The result is all out war from the beginning of the season to the very last regular season game. The two playoff games for the League's championship are like Armageddon I and II.

Due to the fierce competitiveness of the regular season and the state playoffs, rarely does a Mississippi Juco team escape the season without a loss. When a team from the League is undefeated it's because they are extraordinarily good.

Following World War II, junior colleges throughout the U.S. attracted a number of military veterans who had endured the perils and hardships of war. Many of the GIs enrolling in the colleges and universities across the country had seen combat and were hardened war veterans. Consequently, the influx of veterans changed the culture of campus life and the rules of athletic competition.

The older, tougher and more aggressive men no longer fit the pre-war prototype of a typical high school graduate, but were readily embraced by the Juco football coaches in Mississippi. Along with this influx of a new breed of Juco players came a group of battle hardened coaches. Many of these coaches served as officers and drill instructors during their military service. Both players and coaches had learned about the limits of humanity during the war.

The League had always been famous, or infamous, for its rugged style of football, but the influx of war veterans upped the ante. The League became even rowdier. Consider the recollections of a former Juco player, Jesse Murphree, "The hardest I had been hit in my life was when I played Juco ball. When we played in some places it was almost like legal dirty football. It was like a blood bath, both games and practice."

James Sloan, a former Juco player and head coach, describes an experience he had during a game, "I remember playing in a game at Scooba. I got knocked out of bounds on their sideline and ended up under one of their benches. I was trying to crawl out from under there when I heard the other team's coach yelling to his players, 'Don't let him out of there, get him.' That's when the brawl started."

Former head coach of the Ole Miss Rebels, Billy Brewer, recalls watching the annual grudge match between East Mississippi and the Warrior's from East Central. Brewer says, "After the East Central team had completed their warm-up exercises and had gone to their sideline prior to the kickoff, the East Mississippi team finally came onto the field. Half of the team entered the stadium from the north end zone and half from the south. Both groups lined up at the goal lines and started running toward the 50 yard line. They picked up speed and collided at midfield like battering rams or mountain goats. It was like a train wreck. The other team just stood and watched in disbelief."

By no means did any one coach in the league have an exclusive on crazy. The league has always been a treasure trove of flamboyant gridiron generals. However, underneath the veneer of "crazy" another adjective is frequently used to describe Mississippi's Juco coaches--genius. The League has always been noted for its innovations associated with the game it so passionately embraces.

Names of Juco coaches such as Dobie Holden, Sim Cooley, the Delta Fox Jim Randall, Bull Cyclone Sullivan, Goat Hale, H.L."Hook" Stone, Joe Renfroe and A.J. Kilpatrick are spread throughout the annuls of the League. The record books bulge even more when considering the accomplishments of Bobby Ray Franklin, Parker Dykes, Billy Ward, Mike Eaton, Wooky Gray, Gene Murphy, James Sloan, Hugh Shurdon and George Sekul. And coming up right behind these icons are yet another generation of Juco field generals who will add to the legacy of the League.

There are 69 junior college football programs in 17 states of the United States. Mississippi has 14 programs, more than any other state. On a per capita basis, Mississippi has twice the number of Juco football programs as does the next most active state. Mississippi has so many Juco football programs that each one plays its complete schedule entirely against Juco teams from Mississippi.

Mississippi's junior colleges are each supported by public funds from the counties within their defined district. The district lines are based on antiquated legislation that has little or nothing to do with current county population or economic growth.

Each junior college is allowed 55 players on its roster. Of those 55, only 8 can be from out of state. When recruiting begins, each school can place 22 high school players from the counties in its district on a protected list. This means if Hinds puts Mike Jones from Provine High School on its protected list, and Mike decides he wants to play junior college football in Mississippi, he must go to Hinds. If a school chooses not to place a particular player from its district on the protected list, then that player may be recruited by any junior college and may choose to play for a school other than the one in his home district.

Junior colleges in Mississippi, now referred to as community colleges, except for Jones County Junior College, give kids the opportunity to obtain two years of college education at a price significantly less than the cost of a senior college. The average tuition and fees for one semester of community college classes is $1,356. By comparison, the average semester at one of Mississippi's senior colleges is $3,802. The price of community college tuition provides an educational opportunity to kids and families who otherwise might be excluded from higher learning altogether.

Anyone who has graduated high school or passed a high school equivalency exam may enroll in a community college. The applicant does not have to score in a certain percentile on the ACT or the SAT. In fact, neither test has to be taken at all. For high school students who have not yet fully developed their academic skills, the local community college provides them a path for continuing academic growth and development.

Community colleges present wonderful opportunities to Mississippi's high school football players. For the many high school players who are an inch too short or a step to slow to attract the interest of a senior college, the community college league allows them to extend their playing careers. Some of the players who choose this route play two years of Juco ball and simply consider themselves lucky to have enjoyed a prolonged career. However, some players who enter the Juco system find their bodies and skills transformed by the additional two years of experience and then enjoy being courted by the same senior colleges that shunned them a mere 24 months earlier.

In this sense, Mississippi's community colleges provide a mechanism by which the state can incubate and grow its football preemies until they are ready to be unleashed into the mainstream college football world. Consequently, the same athlete in a neighboring state without Juco football would have been forced to accept his status as "not good enough" out of high school and thus the conclusion of his football career.

Love it or hate it, Mississippi Juco football is unique. The League, while considered by some to be rogue, has produced literally thousands of players who have gone on to compete at the Division I and professional levels. Hidden in all the glamor of big-time college and professional football are the staggering number of high school and college coaches produced by the Juco system. Not much attention is given to the players who ended their playing careers at the Juco level but used their experience to advance their skills as coaches. Additionally, little attention is given to the student side of the player's experience. For many of the players in the past, as it is today, Juco ball allowed them an opportunity to continue their education simply because it was financially affordable. After completing two years of community college, many of the students, whether or not they continue to play football, go on to complete their degree requirements at four year colleges and universities.

The League requires a tough player and an even tougher coach. Play calling is aggressive and big hits are the norm. Brawls are not uncommon. Each game is a rivalry or grudge match of some sort. Combine the average Juco player's desire to succeed with a few other choice ingredients unique to Mississippi's Juco system, and the end product is the "Toughest Football League in America."

Members of the League

North Division:

        Northwest Mississippi Community College

        Itawamba Community College

        Northeast Mississippi Community College

        Holmes Community College

        Coahoma Community College

        Mississippi Delta Community College

        East Mississippi Community College

South Division:

        Jones County Junior College

        Mississippi Gulf Coast Community College

        Southwest Mississippi Community College

        Copiah-Lincoln Community College

        Pearl River Community College

East Central Community College

Hinds Community College

In the landmark legislation of 1928, which provided for the establishment of junior colleges in Mississippi, there was a clause that also provided
that "... if a separate school district containing a population of not less than
ten thousand...may extend the curriculum in the school or schools under their
charge so as to include the studies of the freshman or sophomore year or both."

Meridian Junior College, now known as Meridian Community College, is unique among Mississippi's public community colleges as the only
municipally governed college in the state.

Meridian Municipal Junior College opened the 13th grade in 1937
with an enrollment of 132 students. Until 1964, emphasis was given to achieving a closely unified four year program in grades 11-14. In 1956 the local
Negro school T.J. Harris Junior College was merged into Meridian Junior College. In 1964 Meridian Junior College entered a new phase of community
service as a separate unit free from the limitations of the four year educational
plan previously adopted.

While Meridian Community College is a member of the Mississippi
Association of Community and Junior Colleges, it does not participate in athletic competition with fellow members, although it did do so for a brief period from 2003 to 2008. The major reason for Meridian's non-participation
in MACJC athletics is its unlimited recruiting borders. While its 14 sister
schools are confined to legislated districts, Meridian has always embraced a
more regional philosophy when it comes to recruiting students and athletes.

Meridian's cosmopolitan attitude toward recruiting is probably a consequence of the origin of the school as the only municipal junior college in
the Mississippi junior college educational system. The forerunner to the other
junior colleges in the MACJC was the agricultural high school. Consequently, the initial development of the schools started on two somewhat different
tracks--Meridian being more municipal minded, while the others were more
rural oriented. Today, these generalizations are somewhat blurred and only

offer a partial explanation for Meridian's separation from athletic competition within the MACJC.

Originating from these two distinct philosophical tracks an interesting anomaly developed. Meridian is the only member of the MACJC that does not field a football team. This anomaly is even more bizarre when one considers several facts. Take for instance the location of Meridian Community college. Meridian, "The Queen City," is synonamous with football. The Meridian High School Wildcats have amassed an amazing 22 state football championships. No Mississippi high school has a more storied past when it comes to football excellence than Meridian. Of all the places in Mississippi, the mere location of a college in Meridian should automatically generate a winning football program.

To add to the irony, Meridian has Ray Stadium. In 1936, the city built this colossal structure with concrete stands that seats almost 15,000 people. No high school stadium in Mississippi during the '30s came close to matching the size of Ray Stadium. Even more impressive is the fact that no high school stadium in the next 80 plus years in Mississippi would equal the size of "Ray."

To complete the irony of Meridian Community College not fielding a football team is the school's president, Dr. Scott Elliott. "No doubt, my favorite sport is football. My son, Scotty, played quarterback at West Lauderdale, then went on to play two years at East Mississippi, and then completed his career at Mississippi College," says President Elliott.

How strange can it get? Meridian Community College is located in arguably the city with the most storied high school football past and present, the presence of one of the most famous football stadiums in the state, a president whose favorite sport is football, and who sent his own son to a competitor institution so he could play football, so how on earth could Meridian Community College *not* have a team?

Notwithstanding the absence of a football team, the Meridian Community College Eagles have developed their own unique athletic history that sets them apart from the other members of the League. Consider a sampling of some of the Eagles' sports statistics. The MCC baseball team has made appearances in the Juco World Series in 1993, 1994, 1996, 1998, 2000, 2003 and 2004. The MCC golf team was the NJCAA National Champions runners-up in 1998 and 2010. The Eagles' men's soccer team was the 2000 Division I National Champion and has won eight Region 23 championships. The women's soccer team won the MACJC State Championships in 2007, 2008 and 2009 along with Region 23 championship in the same years.

The MCC tennis teams have also contributed to the Eagles athletic legacy by making national junior college tournament appearances in 2002, 2003, 2004, 2005, 2006, 2007, 2008 and 2009. In addition, the men's cross country, indoor track and field and women's slow pitch softball teams have captured championship trophies in recent years.

The result--five NJCAA National Championship titles.

EAGLES TRIVIA:

MCC is the only Mississippi community college to: win a NJCAA men's soccer championship, produce a track Olympian, produce a nine-time state amateur golf champion and produce a Cy Young Award winner.

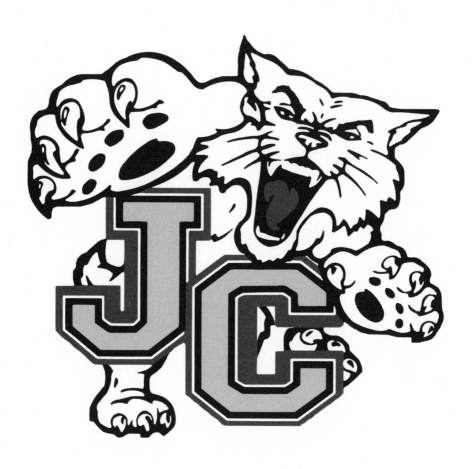

JONES COUNTY JUNIOR COLLEGE

Ellisville, Mississippi • Founded 1927 • Enrollment 6,000

Maroon & Gold • Bobcats

Bobcat Stadium • Capacity 5,500

Marching Band: The Maroon Typhoon

//

THE FREE STATE OF JONES

//The Free State of Jones," myth or reality? The answer depends on who you ask. Some historians believe the label associated with Jones County, Mississippi may have predated the Civil War. This point of view becomes important when considering the current theories regarding the origin of the term. While some of these speculations are certainly plausible from a historical standpoint, other explanations seem somewhat dubious even though colorful and quite entertaining.

In 1826, the Mississippi Legislature formed Jones County by carving out parts of neighboring Wayne and Covington Counties. During the early days after formation of the county, it remained sparsely populated and growth came slowly. For several years after it was established, there were not enough residents in the county to even require an organized local government. As Jones County did start to attract more residents they were not fond of any form of governmental authority or control (i.e. taxes). This tenuous situation persisted until the late 1830s and early '40s when many of the population in the county moved west due to harsh economic conditions. What little organized local government that had been installed started to fall apart due to a shrinking tax base. Consequently, the remaining folks in Jones County slipped back into the previous mindset of "we don't want or need government telling us what to do." At this point in the mid 1840s the county was left without duly inducted legal and civil authorities. It was during this time of lawlessness that the term "Free State of Jones" was first used to describe Jones County.

Recently another theory regarding the origin of the term has emerged. This new theory revolves around the Civil War era and a resident of nearby Jasper County, Newt Knight. The Knight theorists speculate that he deserted the Confederate Army, returned to Jones County to organize a band of fellow deserters and rallied anti-confederate sentiments of the locals to secede from the state of Mississippi, which automatically meant secession from the Confederacy. Knight established a government in, and only for, Jones County, independent of all state, federal and confederate control.

As the tale goes, Knight went on a rampage against.... well, that's where the story proliferates in several directions, and depending on which historian, or movie producer, you wish to believe, you can adopt any number of endings to the Knight saga. For instance, some historians depict Knight as a Robin Hood type figure crediting him with ending Con-

UNFORGETTABLE MOMENT
DECEMBER 1955

JUNIOR ROSE BOWL PITS JONES AGAINST COMPTON IN HISTORIC CLASH:

The Compton Tartars delighted 57,132 fans, the largest crowd in the Junior Rose Bowl history, by defeating the boys from Ellisville, Mississippi, 22-13, in the tenth renewal of the Bowl.

From the time Compton struck first on a 74-yard end around in the first period, action was hot and furious. Four of the five touchdowns were garnered on long distance strikes.

Three TDs were notched in the final two minutes of the first half. Jones QB, Ken Schulte, connected with a 68-yard pass to Ronnie Williams for a tying tally, but the Tartars' Neal Wagerle put Compton out in front to stay by returning the kickoff 86-yards for a score. After recovering a Jones fumble the Tartars tallied on the last play of the half on a QB sneak.

Schulte hit Williams on a 59-yard pass late in the third period to cut the Compton lead, but the Tartars dropped QB Schulte for a safety in the fourth quarter to protect their lead and preserve a hard fought 22-13 victory.

federate control of Jones County during the war. Other experts portray Knight as a deserter, outlaw and the assassin of Jones County native, Major Amos McLemore. Regardless of which version of the Newt Knight story you believe, if any of them, the label "Free State of Jones" is inseparably linked to him and Jones County.

The brief discussion about the background of the term "Free State of Jones" is important because it does relate to the topic of this chapter--Jones County Junior College. From the earliest days of the county's struggling existence it has been populated by independent thinkers who have had a general dislike for authority. During the Civil War era when the popular view was for secession, the Jones County delegation was split on the issue. However, once a decision was made, the residents did their duty on behalf of the Confederacy. Even during the social turmoil of the '50s and '60s, the college carrying the Jones County name made difficult decisions regarding racial issues that were unpopular with many in Mississippi. Today Jones Junior College approaches its mission with the same independent thinking as its residents did back in 1840.

The folks in Jones County, and at Jones County Junior College, do not step aside when confronted with the challenges of life, instead they are known for stepping-up and taking a stand for what they believe is right. Whether people outside the county agree or disagree with the position they take, everyone knows where Jones County folks stand. Independent, self reliant and a "don't tell me what to do" attitude are the traits of the "Free State of Jones" that are still exhibited today at Jones County Junior College.

The college is located in Ellisville, Mississippi. Legend has it that the town was named for Powhatan Ellis, a member of the Mississippi Legislature who claimed to be a direct descendant of Pocahontas. Today the population of Ellisville is approximately 3,500. The spirit of the community personified in the "Free State of Jones" slogan still exists today and is incorporated on patches worn on the uniforms of the sheriff's department personnel.

Ever since the first day that Jones County Junior College started enrolling students in 1927, the college has promoted high standards of academic and athletic excellence befitting the history of the county which it represents with pride.

★ ★ ★ ★ ★

The Junior Rose Bowl began in 1946. Played

in the Rose Bowl stadium in Pasadena, the game pitted the California Junior College football champions against the National Junior College Athletic Association football champions for the mythical junior college national championship.

Four men were primarily responsible for the origin and development of the Junior Rose Bowl. Myron Thomas, President of the Pasadena Junior Chamber of Commerce, rallied the Jaycee members around the project. He selected Walter Hoefflin, later the president of the Tournament of Roses Parade, as his first game chairman. Pus Halbriter of the Signal Youth Foundation provided the financial backing, and energetic Bill Schroeder named a panel of sportswriters to serve on the selection committee and he acted as chairman of the board of management of the game.

However, in 1966 the California Community College Association elected to try a system of state playoff games and, thus, abandoned participation in the Junior Rose Bowl. After a successful run of producing twenty bowl games, the Jaycees were forced to change their format or end the classic. The decision was made to continue under a new name and match two small four-year colleges in the bowl. The Pasadena Bowl was played from 1967 to 1971. The final game in the short life of the new bowl occurred in 1971 when Memphis State defeated San Jose State 28-9.

The state playoff games envisioned by the California Community College Association were financial failures and the system was scrapped. It was obvious that the junior colleges still needed a major showcase for their exciting brand of football. So in 1976 the *Los Angeles Times* assumed the sponsorship of the game in conjunction with the California Community College Association and the Junior Rose Bowl was back in business. That year, Bakersfield, California defeated Ellsworth, Iowa 29-14 before 21,200 fans.

Unfortunately, the renewed life of the Junior Rose Bowl would not be extended for long. The 1977 game would be the last. But, in a strange bit of irony, one of the last two teams to play in the bowl was a team that had played in Pasadena 22 years earlier in front of the largest crowd to ever watch the classic--57,132. The Bobcats of Jones County Junior College from Ellisville, Mississippi had been west before in 1955 and made history in doing so, but not sports history.

In November of 1955, the Bobcats captured their first championship of the Mississippi Junior College Football Conference since 1951. At the same time they completed their first perfect season since 1941. The final 34-12 victory over East Central not only won the conference title for the Bobcats but it also left them in a good position for a possible bid to Pasadena, California's Junior Rose Bowl. The Jones team stood as the only unbeaten junior college team outside of California. In early December 1955, the invitation from the Junior Rose Bowl selection committee came and the Bobcats accepted. A fund raising campaign to take the Jones band was spearheaded by the Laurel Jaycees and overnight thousands of Bobcat supporters contributed to the cause.

After Jones County Junior College had accepted the post season bowl game invitation in Pasadena, California it was learned that their opponent, No. 1 ranked Compton College, was an integrated team. Immediately, shock waves reverberated throughout Mississippi's white community. Never before had a Mississippi team--college, junior college or high school--competed on the same field, in any sport, against a team with Negro players.

BOBCAT TRIVIA:

The first football field, called "the Rock Pile," was located where the J.B. Young Business and Career Center is now located.

Major Sullens wrote an article in the *Jackson Daily News* stating, "Unless the proposed trip to the so-called Junior Rose Bowl is cancelled, a determined effort would be made at the approaching session of the Mississippi Legislature to eliminate Jones County Junior College from the biennial appropriations for junior colleges."

Lieutenant Governor Carroll Gartin, an alumnus of Jones, announced he would not attend the game in Pasadena. The Citizens' Councils announced that a move of this nature would be the opening wedge to bringing on integration. Governor-elect J.P. Coleman declined comment, stating it was a matter for the Junior College board of trustees.

Politics aside, the Jones players never considered anything other than playing against Compton in the bowl game. Kenneth Schulte, co-captain of the football team and president of the sophomore class, was quoted in the *Laurel Leader-Call* saying, "As long as the rules of junior colleges say that

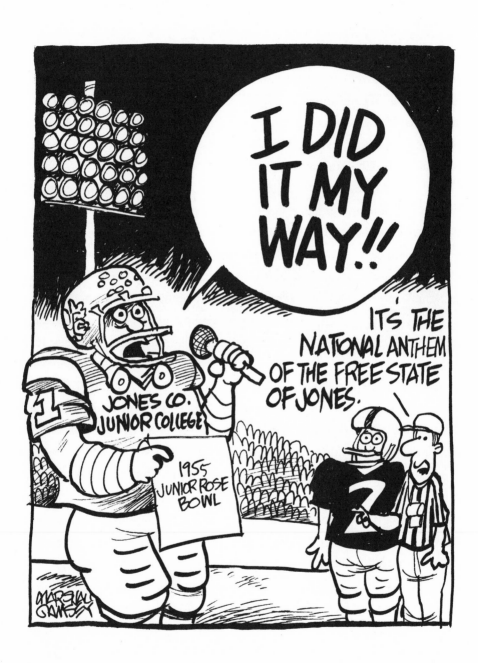

Negroes can play, we're gonna play 'em. I feel that each Negro is just another ball player and we are not worried about who is on the team. We're just going out there to play football."

Paul Hathcock, the other co-captain, said, "It's just another team to me. It's an honor to play in the Junior Rose Bowl and I have no objection whatever to playing against a team that has Negroes on it."

Plans for the game were never altered or cancelled. The Laurel Jaycees completed the fund raising drive to finance the band's trip to Pasadena. While the Jones County Junior College community was solid in its decision to play the game, it met with a firestorm of criticism for its stand. The Covington County Board of Supervisors withdrew its support for the Jones College band, but the $250 donation was replaced by the Chamber of Commerce of Pomona, California. An editorial in the *Jackson Daily News* wished the Jones team would be defeated, stating, "A defeat will not cause mourning in our home state...nothing but avarice and a cold-blooded greed for a share of the receipts could have prompted such action."

On December 6, 1955, the 37-man team and the 110-piece band, along with school officials, left for Pasadena. Six days after their arrival, the Bobcats participated in what was to go down in the records of the Junior Rose Bowl as the most thrilling game ever played in the storied history of this post-season series. The game was played in front of 57,320 spectators, the largest crowd in the Bowl's history. There were no incidents...it was just another football game.

★ ★ ★ ★ ★

Upon the fortieth anniversary of the historic game in Pasadena, the 1955 Jones Bobcats and the Compton Tartars were reunited and honored on the Jones campus during Homecoming 1995. The reunion was covered by *ESPN* and featured on *SportsCenter* along with several major newspapers including the *Philadelphia Inquirer*, the *Washington Post* and the *Los Angeles Times*. The impact of that event so many years ago still resonates with the people at the college and in Jones County. Why?

Perhaps it is because the decision to play that game amidst the public criticism and scorn was so typically Jones, both its county and college. The independent mindset of the people living in this small corner of the world that originated in the 1800s simply has not changed. The game against Compton was played despite the pressure to avoid competing against an integrated opponent simply because the folks in Jones County wanted to do it. To them it was not necessary to offer any reason or excuse, and certainly unnecessary to obtain anyone's permission. The Free State of Jones was free to decide for itself and that's what it did.

Jesse Smith, the current President of Jones County Junior College, was not born when the Bobcats played in the Junior Rose Bowl in 1955. When he was a student in Ellisville he was vaguely aware of the criticism surrounding the Bobcat's trip to Pasadena. He liked the fact the college and its football team had ignored the politically correct view of the world at the time and adopted a "think for yourself" attitude. This Jonesian attitude was further demonstrated to Smith as a member of the Bobcat football team.

> ### UNFORGETTABLE MOMENT
> ### DECEMBER 1977
>
> **JONES JUNIOR COLLEGE AND PASADENA CITY COLLEGE CLASH IN JUNIOR ROSE BOWL:**
>
> The 23rd renewal of the Junior Rose Bowl was played Saturday afternoon (December 10,1977) in the Rose Bowl in Pasadena, California. A crowd of 35,000 watched the Pasadena City College Lancers and the Jones County Junior College Bobcats vie for a possible national title. A surprisingly strong running game propelled the Lancers to a 38-9 win over Jones earning Pasadena the national junior college championship.

Smith learned about how the Jones attitude influenced the way you approached athletic contests, especially football, which in many ways serves as a microcosm for life. In particular he remembers the night in 1995 when the Hinds Junior College Eagles flew into Bobcat Stadium. The Eagles were flying mighty high admiring their No. 1 ranking in the polls and gloating over their 9-0 record. The powerhouse Hinds team was in Ellisville to wrap up a perfect regular season and get on with post season play. To make the situation even worse for the Bobcat faithful, *ESPN* was filming the game to complete an upcoming television special on the success story of the Eagles' dynamic husband and wife coaching duo, Gene and Dot Murphy.

Smith recalls, "During pre-game warmups the Hinds team started chanting 'party time in Ellisville' and acting real confident about the outcome of the game. It really made our crowd angry. The Hinds players continued their chant but our cheerleaders started yelling back and before you knew it all of our fans were worked up. When the two teams ran onto the field to start the game the atmosphere was electric. Because our record that year was only average we had nothing to lose. Coach Dykes must have called every trick play in our playbook. On fourth down and long just inside the Eagles 40-yard line, Coach Dykes took an intentional delay of game penalty to make it appear we were setting up to punt the ball out of bounds. Instead we went for it and made the first down. It was exhilarating whipping Hinds that night. What a feeling!"

The same "don't tell me what to do" attitude that the Jones football team displayed in 1955 was repeated by the 1995 Bobcat team against the No. 1 ranked Eagles. The Jones mindset is not confined to just the football team, it is prevalent throughout the campus and the community. Take for instance President Smith's initiative to provide every student at Jones with an eReader. This initiative enjoyed the successful launch of its pilot version during the fall semester of 2011. No more text books for students to lug around, they will all have state-of-the-art electronic devices. Another example of the progressive Jones attitude in action.

President Smith is also excited about implementing a new system of student government. The new system will resemble a town, complete with a city council, mayor, budget and court system. Smith believes this approach to student government will provide students more interaction with solving the real world issues they will face after college. Yet another example of the same progressive, forward thinking mindset that has characterized the college since it was founded.

The "Free State of Jones" attitude was clearly on display when all of Mississippi's junior colleges elected to change their names to "community colleges." There was only one dissenter. Today, Jones County Junior College remains the state's only public "junior college." Critics of Jones' decision will say they didn't change to community college just to be obstinate. However, Jones' supporters will disagree, stating there was no reason for a name change because the term "junior college" suits them just fine – thank you!

EPIC G★MES

JONES 25
EAST CENTRAL 20

Ellisville, MS, 1983:

In 1983, in the Bobcats' final South Division game at home against East Central with the playoffs on the line, the fans were treated to a thriller. The teams exchanged the lead five times during the contest. The Bobcats were clinging to a 19-17 lead late in the fourth quarter when East Central kicked a 21-yard field goal putting the Warriors on top 20-19.

Working out of the shotgun formation, Bobcat quarterback David Hopper set up to pass, but suddenly tucked the ball and headed straight up the middle and then veered down the left sideline and went untouched into the end zone for the winning points with one second remaining on the clock. The Bobcats won 25-20.

After the win against East Central, Jones went on to win four more games. In the final game of the regular season the Bobcats defeated Coahoma, then blasted Northwest in the first round of the playoffs. In the state championship game in Pascagoula the Bobcats avenged an early season loss with a 17-12 win over Gulf Coast to win the title.

The state championship victory earned Jones the right to host Harford Community College (Maryland) in the East Bowl. The Bobcats won 34-14 over the heavily favored and previously unbeaten Owls.

The Bobcats finished the season 11-2, the second most wins in a season ever recorded in Bobcat football history. One play, lasting 10 seconds and covering 52 yards, made the difference in a decent season and a championship season.

JONES' HEAD COACH ROSTER

J.W. Elmore 1929-1930

Bill Denson 1931-1936

John Read 1937-1944

Melvin Vines 1945-1946

B.L. "Country" Graham 1947-1949

Paul Davis 1950-1954

Jim Clark 1955-1956

Milton White 1957-1958

A.B. Howard 1959-1960

Sim Cooley 1961-1987

Elmer Higginbotham 1988-1991

Parker Dykes 1992-2005

Eddie Pierce 2006-present

Sim Cooley

Eddie Pierce

JONES' RECRUITING DISTRICT

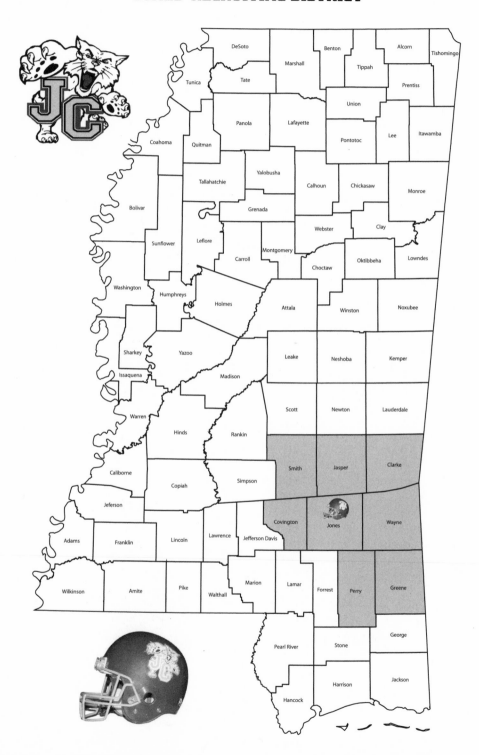

JONES' DISTRICT HIGH SCHOOLS

Enterprise
Quitman
Clarkdale
Collins
Mt. Olive
Seminary
Greene County
Bay Springs
Heidelberg
Heidelberg Academy
Stringer
Sylva-Bay Academy
Laurel
Laurel Christian
Northeast Jones
South Jones
West Jones
Perry Central
Richton
Mize
Raleigh
Taylorsville
Wayne Academy
Wayne County

OFFICIAL PROGRAM

$.4836 Selling Price
.0164 Sales Tax
TOTAL PRICE

50¢

Tenth Annual

JUNIOR ROSE BOWL GAME

SPONSORED BY PASADENA JUNIOR CHAMBER OF COMMERCE

Jones Junior College
ELLISVILLE, MISSISSIPPI
VS.
Compton College
COMPTON, CALIFORNIA

SATURDAY, DECEMBER 10, 1955 — 1:30 P.M.

HINDS COMMUNITY COLLEGE

Raymond, Mississippi • Founded 1922 • Enrollment 19,500

Maroon & White • Eagles

Joe Renfroe Stadium • Capacity 6,000

Marching Band: Eagle Marching Band

Chapter
3

//

A PINK METAL ELEPHANT

Legend has it that Bozo arrived on the Hinds campus sometime in the mid-40s. While there is no evidence to pinpoint the exact date of Bozo's arrival, or birth, albeit whatever manner he, she or it, was created, the date of its origin still remains a mystery. There is some sketchy data indicating that Bozo and its descendants, Bozo II and Bozo III continued to reside in and around the Raymond area until the '70s. But again, credible information regarding the Bozo clan's dates of comings and goings at Hinds is nonexistent.

After decades of investigation by local historians, amateur sleuths and several law enforcement agencies, some credible facts, although still quite hazy, have slowly emerged about the metal pachyderm and its offspring. For reasons that remain unknown, Bozo was at the center of numerous brawls between students at Hinds and their counterparts at Holmes Junior College in Goodman, Mississippi. Oddly, the brawls inspired by Bozo always occurred in the fall before, after or during football games between the two schools. Why, or how, Bozo was able to instigate such violent behavior between the Hinds and Holmes students remains one of the many unanswered questions surrounding the mascot's mysterious powers.

Journals kept by some students at Hinds during the "reign of Bozo" indicate that it was originally used as a porch ornament, or doorstop, at the old Shangri-La athletic dormitory. But due to Bozo's powerful influence on the Hinds campus, it became the target of night raids by Juco terrorists, especially those located in Goodman who attended Hinds' arch rival institution, Holmes Junior College. Holmes students took great delight in kidnapping Bozo and removing it to Goodman, or some other unknown destination, for imprisonment. Sometimes Bozo would remain a captive for a few weeks, months or for several years. During those times Bozo was held captive, Hinds students would plot rescue operations to regain possession of their beloved metal mascot. Unfortunately, the custody battle over Bozo got ugly in 1954.

Apparently, early in the week of the Holmes-Hinds football game some Holmes students, although such accusations are unverifiable by any credible witnesses, stole Bozo and retreated back to Goodman with their prize. A group of outraged Hinds students traveled to Goodman, slipped into the dormitory where Bozo was being held captive and rescued it from its captors. Bozo was returned to Raymond and provided 24/7 security.

> ## UNFORGETTABLE MOMENT
> ## 1957
>
> ### SPECTACULAR SEASON:
>
> Although without the fanfare of the 1954 Junior Rose Bowl Champions, the 1957 Eagles squad was arguably at least an even match. The Eagles' only scare of the season came in the opener, a 35-32 win over Pearl River Junior College. Hinds outscored the next nine opponents 283-14 with seven shutouts, an average margin of victory of 30 points while allowing an average of 1.5 points. The closest contest was a 20-7 win over Jones County Junior College.

Several days later during the football game between the two schools near halftime Hinds students, probably the rescue team, proudly displayed Bozo and paraded it around the track. All hell broke loose. Students from both schools rushed from the stands to the track and a full scale brawl started. At the center of the melee' stood Bozo. Like a general of an ancient army leading his warriors into battle, Bozo a la Caesar, Alexander the Great, or from the Holmes' students perspective Hannibal, was leading the charge to combat.

Earl Leggett, Hinds player, witnessed the "battle for Bozo" on that Saturday afternoon in the fall of '54. He recalls, "It was the darndest thing you've ever seen. We watched the fight for about five minutes. It must have been 150 kids out there fighting. It was brutal. It's a miracle nobody got hurt."

The Hinds army prevailed that glorious day in 1954. The Holmes barbarians were repelled and the Hinds warriors were able to fend off another kidnapping attempt of their beloved mascot. It appeared that Bozo would continue its reign over the Raymond campus and all would be right in the Juco world. Sadly, such would not be Bozo's destiny.

Several of Hinds' school officials were not amused with the cult like power Bozo seemed to have over the students of both schools. Secretly, a plot was concocted to dispose of Bozo...forever. One of the Hinds' officials who allegedly masterminded the insidious plot, and whose identification has been kept secret due to possible retaliation from the "followers of Bozo", took the metal elephant into so called protective custody after the fight was brought under control.

The plan was to transport Bozo under cover of darkness to Raymond Lake. The unnamed assassin, who obviously had the help of one or more co-conspirators, loaded Bozo into a motorboat and proceeded to the middle of the lake and then dumped the campus icon into its watery grave. After the deadly plot was completed darkness fell over the Hinds campus with the strange disappearance of Bozo.

Hinds students suspected foul play. Of course at the center of their suspicion was anyone who was remotely affiliated with the low life bunch in Goodman. Then in 1957 a startling chain of events took place that shook the Hinds community like an earthquake.

In 1957, Raymond Lake was drained so that needed repairs and improvements could be made. As the water level slowly receded an object in the middle of the lake started to appear. There it was.....Bozo!

Like a conquering general returning to his homeland after being away for a three year campaign in foreign lands, Bozo made a triumphant return to the Hinds campus. While the Hinds students were thrilled to see the return of the famous pink metal elephant many students wondered, "Who was responsible for the attempted murder of Bozo?" Suspicion was at a fever pitch. Was it the scoundrels at Holmes, or maybe, just maybe, was it an inside job?

One witness brave enough to speak out about the events after Bozo

was exhumed from the murky depths of Raymond Lake was Amos Jack (AJ) Gray. AJ was the sophomore class president in the fall of 1957. According to AJ, "After Bozo returned from the dead there were a lot of questions regarding his disappearance. Then it happened. Holmes students kidnapped Bozo yet again. Once safely back in Goodman they put Bozo on display in the cafeteria for public ridicule. However, within hours, Hinds students were developing a rescue plan. Later, in the early morning hours, a group of brave Hinds operatives penetrated the cafeteria at Holmes and started a precision rescue operation of Bozo. While securing custody of the steel prize a night-watchman discovered the break in security and went to alert his back-up troops. During the critical minutes following their discovery in the cafeteria by the enemy

guard, the rescuers pushed Bozo through a cafeteria window, loaded it in their vehicle and raced to Raymond without being captured by the Goodman police."

AJ continues, "It happened again at halftime of the Hinds-Holmes football game the following week at Goodman. One of the rockets in the fireworks display misfired and landed close to the Hinds band. Thinking that they were under rocket attack by Holmes sympathizers, the Hinds students sought a counter force and rolled out Bozo. Its presence lead to another out right brawl. After law and order were restored, Holmes school officials demanded that Bozo be removed from the premises."

Fearing further kidnapping attempts by Holmes students, Bozo was quickly removed from the stadium under heavy guard and transported out of enemy territory by a caravan of loyalists.

The saga of Bozo was not over. According to AJ, "I offered to keep Bozo at my house the night after the big fight. But the next morning I discovered that it had been stolen from my car. To this day, Bozo has never been found."

Many rumors supported by nothing but high speculation continue to swirl around the disappearance of Bozo in 1957. One such story links a telephone call made by Hinds president, George McLendon (Mr. Mac), to the president of Holmes, Frank Branch, on Monday following the incident in Goodman. During this conversation Branch was purportedly told by Mr. Mac that if the mascot reappeared, Hinds would cut it into little pieces and throw them into the Big Black River.

We will never know if Bozo met such a horrible fate because it never reappeared. Mysteriously, the great metal mascot, or as the Goodmanites refer to it, the beast, has remained hidden from public view since that fateful day in 1957.

Another story that still lingers as part of the Bozo lore is that Coach Joe Renfroe knew of Bozo's final resting place. There was speculation that on the 25th anniversary of Hinds' 1954 National Championship he would reveal the sacred site. When the 25th anniversary was celebrated Coach Renfroe either chose not to reveal the location of Bozo's remains or was as clueless as everyone else.

Adding some credibility to Renfroe's recollection is the fact he had a replica of Bozo signed by his 1954 team, coupled with statements made by him in private that he felt the mascot enjoyed a "respectable resting place."

> ## UNFORGETTABLE MOMENT
> ## DECEMBER 1988
>
> ### HINDS VS HOLMES FOR STATE CHAMPIONSHIP:
>
> It had been 31 years since Hinds had celebrated the victory of a state championship but the opportunity had finally arrived. Even though the game was played under horrible weather conditions, and with the emotional strain brought about by the death of a player on each team during the season, the game was a classic. In the end Hinds prevailed 25-20 over the Holmes Bulldogs. Coach Gene Murphy said, "This was the toughest team I have ever coached."

The legend of Bozo doesn't end in 1957. At some unknown date after the departure of Bozo the Great, a smaller wooden version of the mascot, named Bozo II, emerged. But Bozo II suffered the same mysterious fate as his predecessor, vanishing without a trace just months after its arrival.

According to an article that appeared in a 1974 edition of the *Hindsonian*, another metal monster named Bozo III appeared on the scene circa 1965. This iteration of the beloved mascot also vanished shortly after its arrival. When Raymond Lake was drained for the first time since 1957 it happened again. Bozo III emerged from the waters. But, like a Houdini magic show,

Bozo III also vanished under the same strange circumstances as its predecessors. Three Bozos and three mysterious disappearances.

While it cannot be confirmed, because nothing about the dynasty of the Bozos can be verified, the famous author of *Chariots of the Gods*, Eric VonDaniken, has been rumored to be investigating the strange, unexplainable events surrounding the disappearance of the three Bozos. Even more mysterious than their disappearance is the incredible, almost supernatural power the objects wielded over the students at Holmes and Hinds. Could it be that the Bozos', particularly Bozo the Great, the first mascot, origin was from another world? We await the completion of VonDaniken's investigation and the publication of his next book with hopes he will explain the mysteries.

From the first time Hinds fielded a true "junior college" football team (circa 1926), the Eagles have always been supported by the school's marching band. Ever since the '30s the Hinds band has featured majorettes. In the late '40s the majorettes started making a transition to becoming more of a precision dance and drill team with their own name. In 1949, the Hinds Hi-Steppers, the third oldest precision drill team in the nation, officially came into existence as part of the Eagle Marching Band.

Recognizing that dance and drill teams were becoming very popular, a group of dance team and band members from Hinds visited the Kilgore Junior College Rangerettes, who at the time were making a name for themselves nationally as the premier college dance and drill team. After visiting with the Rangerettes, the Hi-Steppers revamped their routine adopting many of Kilgore's innovative techniques, plus adding their own flair for dance, and quickly started to gain statewide and regional attention. The Hi-Steppers made their first out-of-state appearance on New Years Day in 1952 at the Oleander Bowl in Galveston, Texas when Hinds played San Angelo Junior College.

Despite having gained a regional reputation by 1953, the fame of the Hi-Steppers as a national attraction was just beginning. Starting her employment at Hinds in 1953 as the director of the Hi-Steppers, Anna Cowder Bee, or Mrs. Bee, became the personification of the group. Mrs. Bee brought a performance background in dance to the director position and made the job a full time endeavor. The performance skills and uniqueness of the Hi-Steppers routines launched the group into international stardom.

The Hi-Steppers have performed across the United States, Canada and Europe. The group has performed for U.S. presidents, multiple Super Bowl audiences and attended numerous dance reviews worldwide. The Hi-Steppers have been featured in *National Geographic* and *Time* magazines and CBS television network. The Hinds Hi-Steppers are known as Mississippi's Goodwill Ambassadors. In 2003, Mrs. Bee celebrated her 50th year as director of the Hi-Steppers.

Since its inception the Hinds football program has been at the forefront of Juco football in Mississippi and the nation, winning a national championship in 1954.

Archives indicate that Hinds was one of the first junior colleges in Mississippi to field a football team. By 1926 Hinds was a member of the State Junior College Library and Athletic Association. In 1928 the Hinds athletic teams became officially known as the Eagles, and by 1931 Hinds played a football schedule consisting of all junior college teams, no longer competing with freshmen squads at Millsaps and Mississippi College, both private four year schools.

The golden era of Hinds football was between 1951 and 1957 under Coaches Devall and Renfroe (1954). The 1954 campaign culminated in a 13-7 victory over El Camino Junior College in the ninth annual Junior Rose Bowl played in front of 54,633 in the Rose Bowl in Pasadena, California in December 1954. The Williamson Gridiron ratings ranked Hinds number one after the Eagles' win over El Camino and declared Hinds the 1954 Junior College National Champion.

Another interesting part of the Hinds football tradition occurred while Bill Buckner was the head coach. In the fall of 1984, Buckner hired a new receivers coach. So why is that fact so important? Well, the new coach was Dorothy Murphy, Dot for short. Dot became the only female football coach at the college level in the United States.

Dot was an outstanding basketball player in high school, college and played on the U.S. team in the 1973 World Games. She became a women's college basketball coach after her playing days. Dot's husband, Gene, became an assistant on Buckner's staff in 1983 and she temporarily left the work force to raise two small children.

After the 1983 season, Buckner approached Dot about the possibility of her coaching receivers the next year. She found the idea ludicrous, at least at first. Dot became intrigued with the similarities between guarding players and breaking away from coverage in basketball and the role of receivers in football. All her basketball knowledge and experience, movement in space, catching the ball, reacting to zone and man coverage were all applicable to football.

After Buckner's persistence Dot finally agreed to try it. Husband Gene was alright with her giving it a try because he coached on the defensive side of the ball and had little interaction with the offense.

Surprisingly, it worked and Dot was rehired the next year as a full time football coach. Then Gene Murphy became the head football coach succeeding Buckner. The husband and wife coaching partnership lasted for 15 years. During that time the Eagles won six state championships and earned runner-up spots in three others.

Gene and Dot retired from coaching football in 2003. Then, like Bozo the Great, Gene returned as the Eagles head football coach in 2009. As Coach Murphy leads his team into the 2011 season he will have led more gridiron campaigns than any other Hinds football coach.

HINDS COMMUNITY COLLEGE 13
EL CAMINO COLLEGE 7

Pasadena, CA, 1954:

A Junior Rose Bowl crowd of 54,633 was treated to a thriller as the Hinds Junior College Eagles from Raymond, Mississippi and the El Camino College Warriors from El Camino, California battled for the Junior College National Championship.

The game turned on the ability of the Eagles to successfully run the football and play tough defense. Halfback Olin Renfroe dashed 50-yards for a touchdown in the second quarter, but El Camino tied the score at 7 all halfway through the third. Moments later Renfroe answered with a 64-yard sprint. The extra point was botched, however, leaving Hinds with a precarious 13-7 edge. El Camino reached the Hinds 4-yard line at the end of the third quarter, but the Eagle defense held on downs. In the fourth, Hinds drove to the Warriors five with four minutes left in the game, but returned the favor by losing the ball at the nine. The Eagles stuffed the Warriors on their next possession, took over on downs and were at the El Camino 15-yard line when time expired.

HINDS' HEAD COACH ROSTER

George F. McGowan 1926

H.G. Laird 1927-1929

Joe R "Jobie" Harris 1930-1935

Zeus Denton 1936-1937

Bernie Ward 1938

Clyde "Heifer" Stuart 1939-1944

John Read 1945

Les DeVall 1946-1953

Joe Renfroe 1954-1969

Earl Leggett 1970

Durwood Graham 1971-1979

Bill Buckner 1980-1987

Gene Murphy 1988-2002

J. Mike Smith 2003-2008

Gene Murphy 2009-present

Gene Murphy

HINDS' RECRUITING DISTRICT

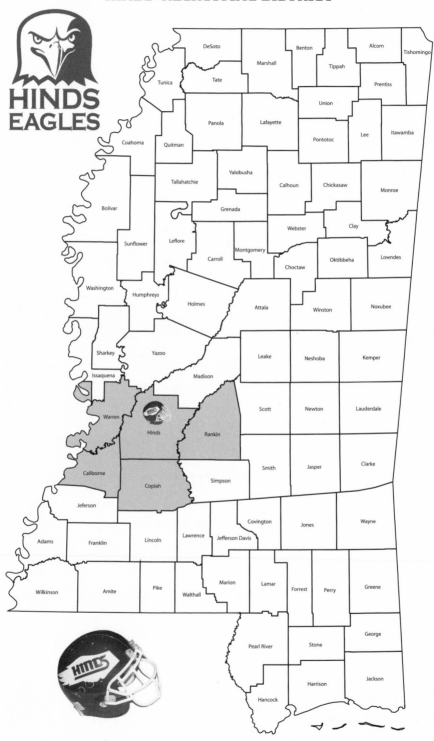

HINDS' DISTRICT HIGH SCHOOLS

Bailey Magnet

Brandon

Callaway

Central Hinds

Chamberlain-Hunt

Clinton

Clinton Christian

East Rankin

Florence

Forest Hill

Hillcrest Christian

Hinds AHS

Jackson Academy

Jackson Prep

Jim Hill

Lanier

McLaurin

MS School for the Deaf

Murrah

Northwest Rankin

Pearl

Pelahatchie

Pisgah

Port Gibson

Porter's Chapel

Provine

Puckett

Raymond

Rebul Academy

Richland

St. Aloysius

Terry

University Christian

Vicksburg

Warren Central

Wingfield

HOLMES COMMUNITY COLLEGE

Goodman, Mississippi • Founded 1925 • Enrollment 6,500

Cardinal, White & Black • Bulldogs

Ras Branch Stadium • Capacity 5,500

Marching Band: The Bulldog Marching Band

Chapter

4

//

DID YOU HEAR THE STORY ABOUT...

Goodmanites are storytellers. Evidence of this fact can be seen in the accomplishments of two of its favorite sons, John A. Lomax (1867-1948), a pioneering folklorist, and David Herbert Donald (1920-2009), a two time Pulitzer prize winning historian and Harvard professor.

From the time the town was founded in 1865 the folks of Goodman have entertained themselves with stories and reports about events and individuals in their small town. One of the primary reasons many of their stories have been preserved is because of one lady, Mrs. Will J. Nelson.

Mrs. Nelson was the organizer and founder of the Woman's Reading Club of Goodman. The club was organized in 1893 and Mrs. Nelson served as its president for nearly thirty years. In 1951, the club helped organize The Magnolia Club, a junior version of the Woman's Reading Club, for the younger women of Goodman.

Both clubs were instrumental in the advancement of the literary culture of Goodman and for the preservation of the stories and news events generated in their town and throughout Holmes County. Because of these two clubs, stories dating back to the early 1900s can still be retold today. Oh, by the way, did you hear the story about the $5.00 gold piece?

After returning from a trip to Memphis, a member of a prominent Goodman family was telling her husband of her experience on the train. She asked the lady sitting next to her to watch her purse while she went to the restroom.

Upon returning, she discovered the five dollar gold piece she always kept in her purse was missing. Later, the seat-mate went to the restroom, making the same request of her. This gave her an opportunity to check the lady's purse. Sure enough, there was a five dollar gold piece, which she promptly took.

Her husband asked if she remembered the lady's name. When she replied in the negative, he said, "Honey, I hate to tell you this, but you stole that woman's gold piece. I took yours out before you left. There it is on the mantle."

Some Goodmanites still remember Paul Waugh's monkey named Billy. At Paul's death, he left the monkey to his good friend Mr. Moss. Apparently, Billy and Mr. Moss became good friends. Sometimes Mr. Moss would go to the beer joints to drink and Billy would go too.

> ## UNFORGETTABLE MOMENT
> ## NOVEMBER 2002
>
> ### BULLDOGS CLAIM STATE CHAMPIONSHIP:
>
> Five takeaways, three huge defensive stops in the waning minutes of the fourth quarter and a 69-yard jaunt by speedy Terrance Fleming tell the story in Holmes' first state football championship since 1981. The 9-2 Bulldogs defeated the 8-3 Jones County Bobcats 7-0 in Ellisville Saturday afternoon in the MACJC title game.

When Billy would get happy, he would not ride inside the car with Mr. Moss, but instead stand on the hood jumping and flapping his arms. The neighbors would see them coming and say, "Billy Moss is drunk again."

One night they were both thrown in jail for public intoxication. The next morning, Mrs. Moss went down and got Billy out of jail. She said, "He didn't know any better." Her husband, however, was left in jail to serve out his fine.

Legendary head football coach and acting athletic director for the Holmes Bulldogs, Hugh Shurden, has inherited the love and ability of Goodmanites to tell spellbinding stories. When Coach Shurden is asked how he describes the town of Goodman to athletic recruits visiting the campus he quickly laughs and skillfully replies, "There is no town." Facing what would appear to be an insurmountable obstacle in trying to lure teenagers to a remote college campus to play football and attend class he confidently says, "Well its how you present the story. First, I never take the recruits downtown. I go in the opposite direction and never mention it. Instead I drive around our beautiful campus and emphasize all the positive features Holmes has to offer. It's all in the story."

Sure enough, once the storyline is properly calibrated and one looks closely at what the little hideaway college has to offer, then one's perspective starts to change. What at first might appear to be a dull, uninspiring, nonfiction story is in reality an action packed adventure novel.

The small intriguing town of Goodman, population of approximately 1,250 when the college is not in session, is located about one hour north of the state capital in Jackson. Goodman is situated in the southeastern part of Holmes County. The town of Durant lies to the North, Pickens to the South, Lexington to the West, and on its eastern border is the Big Black River. Goodman was first chartered in 1865 but lost its charter because of a legal technicality and was rechartered March 5, 1878.

The primary industries in the area are timber, cotton farming and hunting camps. One of the hidden treasures in Holmes County is a $12 million hunting camp offering its members every conceivable modern amenity and convenience.

Once you get off I-55 and turn on to Highway 14 there is nothing but timberland as far as the eye can see. While it is highly unlikely that anyone would haphazardly find their way to Goodman from the outside world, it is quite the opposite for outdoorsmen and folks searching for some solitude. For those visitors wanting to enjoy the treasures Holmes County has to offer, the place is a secret paradise.

It's all in the way the story is presented, and Coach Shurden spins a pretty good one. He points out to the recruits and their parents who visit the 196 acre campus some interesting facts. For instance, there is no traffic congestion, irritating noises or crowded streets to contend with like in the big cities. Goodman is a town where you can still leave the keys in the ignition of

your car and residents rarely think about locking their doors at night. There is no reason to feel threatened because the crime rate is zero.

In addition, the quiet, uncluttered environment in which Holmes is located is very conducive to concentrating on the important aspects of the college experience. The lack of distractions is even more critical to student athletes who must learn how to balance the demands of college academics with the intense training required for highly competitive collegiate sports. Students who are serious about their respective studies and sport quickly learn to appreciate the opportunity provided to them in Goodman.

While studying and playing sports are certainly important aspects of college life, there is another dimension of the college experience that Holmes provides its students. Due to the seclusion of the campus, students spend lots of time with each other, especially during the week. Consequently everyone gets to know each other. After a few weeks students, faculty, staff and the residents of Goodman are connected. In essence, the college and town become one as the population of Goodman doubles in size while classes are in session.

No matter how serious they take their academics and sports, college students need to have their down time. When the outdoor amenities and activities don't fulfill students' recreational urges, the many attractions of the big city one hour to the south fill the void. Jackson provides Holmes students with an endless number of restaurants, clubs, shopping, entertainment and sports events. As Coach Shurden says, "The students at Holmes have the best of both worlds," which of course, leads to another story.

A local resident, Charlie Donald, remembers the night Sue Peel's liquor store burned in January 1975. "It was so cold the firefighters' clothes froze to the ladders they were on." Part of the building and some of the stock were saved. The next day the Alcohol Beverage Control inspector came up and condemned the stock. Charlie said "I knew that was malarkey because, had it been contaminated, half of Goodman would have been dead, including the fire chief."

Today Holmes is the sixth largest community college in the Mississippi system, which consists of fifteen schools. The College achieved dramatic growth by establishing satellite centers in Grenada and Ridgeland. Both operations have grown steadily pushing the Holmes student population up every year.

The Holmes football team also has an interesting legacy. Clearly, one of the most noteworthy statistics regarding the Bulldog football program was recorded in 1950. The state champion Holmes team under Coach J.W. Patrick and Coach Bobby Oswalt played in the sixth annual Lions Bowl Game in Laurel defeating East Mississippi Junior College 46-20. During the next week the Bulldogs played in the Memorial Bowl Game in Jackson and in the Gulf Bowl in Corpus Christi, Texas. Holmes is the only college football team in the United States to play in three bowl games in thirteen days.

The Bulldogs also have the distinction of playing in the first junior college bowl game to be played in the United States. Coach Frank Branch's co-champion Holmes team and Hinds Junior College participated in the Lions Bowl Game in Laurel in 1945. The game ended in a 0-0 tie.

Over the years Bull-dog football teams have won several state championships, the most recent occurring in 2002 under Coach Hugh Shurden. They have also made numerous appearances in post season bowl games.

In the fall, Thurs-day nights and Saturday afternoons are the most popular times of the year at Holmes because that's when the Bulldog football games are played. All the neighborhoods comprising the town of Goodman join forces to show their support for the team. Spectators fill the seats in the stadium to cheer on the Holmes team. In many ways the Thursday night games are a throwback to the time the Branch brothers, Ras and Frank, coached at Holmes in the mid-'30s.

At that time, the Illinois Central railroad ran special trains to Wesson, Mississippi so students and fans could follow their Bulldogs when Holmes played at Copiah-Lincoln and likewise from Wesson to Goodman when the Wolves played at Goodman. The treks to and from Raymond, Mississippi on the "pink elephant" when arch rivals Holmes and Hinds Junior College played were always exciting too. The train to Raymond named "the pink elephant" has yet another story attached to it; for the gorey details refer to chapter three. Yet another eagerly anticipated event was the parading of the big "plantation bell" when Holmes and Mississippi Delta Junior College played each other. The fans' spirit at both schools was always inflamed when "the bell" made an appearance, so much so that the bell had to be retired. During the mid-'30s to the '40s, Holmes fielded powerhouse teams under the Branch brothers winning three state championships.

While the train trips, rides on the pink elephant and exchanging the plantation bell are no longer a part of Holmes' current football traditions, one aspect of its legacy has not fallen to the wayside. The intense, highly competitive, street fighter mentality of the Juco game has not changed.

UNFORGETTABLE MOMENT
NOVEMBER 1950

HOLMES RALLIES TO TOP CO-LIN 34-14 FOR STATE JUCO TITLE:

Highly favored Holmes had to come from behind to defeat their cellar-dwelling old grudge rival, Copiah-Lincoln, but they did so in grand fashion, 34-14, and sewed up the 1950 Mississippi Junior College Championship in Wesson.

Another unique characteristic of the Holmes football program that remains intact today is the makeup of its football team. Except for 6A powerhouse Madison Central and Grenada High School, all the other schools in Holmes' recruiting district are small schools in rural areas. Holmes gets its players from the small towns of Weir, Ackerman, West and Eupora. But, behold the irony of Mississippi high school football, it is these small towns in rural Mississippi that provide the Jucos and major universities across America with some of the greatest football talent every year. NFL Hall of Fame wide receiver Jerry Rice hails from tiny Crawford, Mississippi, just to name one such example.

Consequently year after year the no name players from the small schools in Holmes' district fill the Bulldog roster. From the days of the Branch brothers in the '30s to today when current head coach Jeff Koonz is recruiting, the backbone of the Bulldog teams have always been the same--players from small town Mississippi.

Coach Shurden once asked his Bulldog players a question, "Why do you play the game?" He recalls some of the emotional statements made by former players in response to his question. The responses were quite revealing and heartwarming, which brings to mind yet another memory--another story. "Did anyone tell you about the train trip to Wesson in the late '30s?" asked Coach Shurden.

In the '30s, the railroad would put on an extra train to take loyal Bulldog fans to the Copiah-Lincoln game in Wesson, Mississippi. One of the city fathers took his spirits with him in his hip pocket. The stopper slipped out of the bottle and he felt the cold liquid wetting his seat. One of the teachers across the aisle complained of smelling whiskey. The old gentleman said, "I guess I had better go check on those young boys. You know they will try the stuff."

 EPIC G★MES

LIONS BOWL - DECEMBER 2, 1950
LAUREL, MS

HOLMES JUNIOR COLLEGE	**46**
EAST MISSISSIPPI JUNIOR COLLEG	**20**

MEMORIAL BOWL - DECEMBER 9, 1950
JACKSON, MS

HOLMES JUNIOR COLLEGE	**13**
KILGORE JUNIOR COLLEGE (TX)	**32**

GULF BOWL - DECEMBER 15, 1950
CORPUS CHRISTI, TX

HOLMES JUNIOR COLLEGE	**12**
DEL MAR JUNIOR COLLEGE (TX)	**35**

Holmes coaches J.W. Patrick and Bobby Oswalt led their 1950 State Juco Champion team in three bowl games in one post season. In doing so, Holmes became the only college team in the United States to play in three bowl games in thirteen days.

HOLMES' HEAD COACH ROSTER

Roy Hartness 1928-1929

Ras Branch 1930-1938

Frank Branch 1939-1946

T.F. Binion 1947-1948

Frank Branch 1949

J.W. Patrick 1950-1951

Oliver Poole 1952-1953

Van Stewart 1954-1956

J.W. Patrick 1957

Horace McCool 1958-1959

Billy Mustin 1960-1963

Ken Lauderdale 1964-1965

Robert McGraw 1966-1971

Tommy Davis 1972-1976

Quinby Morgan 1977-1979

A.J. Kilpatrick 1980-1982

Johnny Fulce 1983-1985

Robert Pool 1986-1994

Hugh Shurden 1995-2007

Danny Robertson 2008-2010

Jeff Koonz 2011

Hugh Shurden

HOLMES' RECRUITING DISTRICT

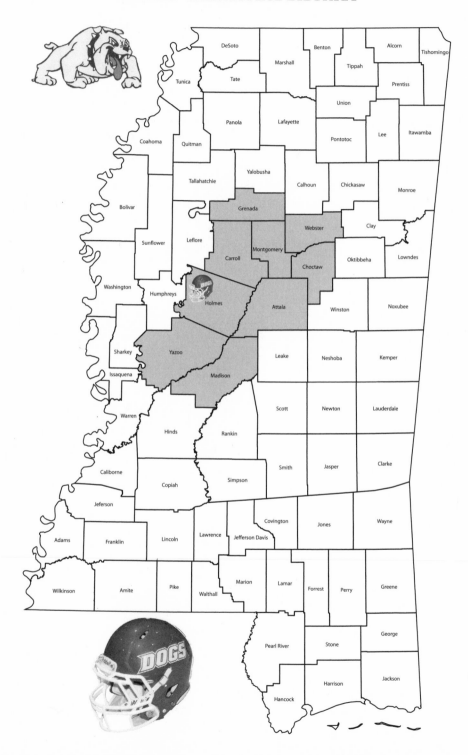

HOLMES' DISTRICT HIGH SCHOOLS

Kosciusko

McAdams

Yazoo County

Ethel

Benton Academy

Montgomery County

Manchester Academy

J.Z. George

St. Joseph - Madison

Winona

St. Andrews

Winona Christian School

Tri-County Academy

Weir

Ackerman

French Camp

Grenada

Kirk Academy

J.J. McClain

S.V. Marshall

Durant

Williams-Sullivan

Central Holmes Christian School

Madison Central

Ridgeland

Germantown

Velma Jackson

Madison-Ridgeland Academy

Canton

Canton Academy

East Webster

Eupora

EAST CENTRAL COMMUNITY COLLEGE

Decatur, Mississippi • Founded 1928 • Enrollment 2,900

Black & Gold • Warriors

Bailey Stadium • Capacity 5,000

Marching Band: The Wall O' Sound

///

WAR DRUMS

Here are two questions to ponder; the answers to both will be revealed later in this chapter. Question number one, "What do East Central and Elvis Presley have in common?" A hint, it has to do with football. The second question, "What do East Central and the Cleveland Browns of the National Football League have in common?" Yes, the answer also has to do with football. Both are thought provoking questions aren't they? But for now, let's go back in time, all the way to the '60s and '70s and even further back to the '40s and '50s. What was Juco football like at East Central during those early days?

Other than old photographs, newspaper articles and school publications we can only view fragments of these times to get some idea of what it was like back then. However, to really enhance our time travel to these by-gone years there are several folks who can assist us in our journey. Hearing from some of the people who were there and took part in the events that make up those by-gone days of Warrior football will help transport us back to that earlier time.

Let's go back on the campus of East Central Junior College in Decatur, the county seat of Newton County, Mississippi, during game week in the late '50s. The constant beating of the war drum signals the approaching enemy and a major battle on the horizon. There is definitely a sense of excitement surrounding the Warrior players at practice the day before the big game. There is an urgency to the coaches' commands to the players as they prepare for the pending battle. In a little over 24 hours, it will start--all out war with EC's long standing arch-rival to the northeast, the East Mississippi Lions from Scooba.

Gaines Massey (1958-59) recalls his arrival on the East Central campus and the fierce battles with the Scooba Lions, " The Korean conflict had ended a few years earlier and following passage of the GI Bill, many veterans came to EC and the other junior colleges. Several of the football players ranged in age from 21 to 26 years old. Some had scars from combat and many had tattoos. There were a lot of rough, tough, mean guys who had been through the horrors of war."

Massey continues, "I felt intimidated by the older players and after talking to some of the former servicemen the night before our first ball practice began, I thought maybe I was in the wrong place. I seriously considered going home that first night, but I couldn't. I did not have a ride back to Morton so I stayed. I'm sure glad I did."

Massey and his teammates compiled a 7-4 record his freshman year. During his freshman season Massey had the distinct pleasure of getting to play in two games against EC's bitter rival, East Mississippi, which at the time was led by their legendary coach, Bull Cyclone Sullivan.

"We won the first game 14-12 in the season opener and then lost the second contest 20-6 later in the year," Massey recalls. "It was a really bitter rivalry back then. One game with them was really one too many."

But the most memorable game against Scooba came his sophomore season in 1959 when the Warriors posted a 6-4 record. The game was played at a neutral site in Meridian. Massey recalls one event quite vividly, "About midway in the first quarter, Coach Sullivan ran on the field and yelled to his players that he wanted me killed. That was a scary feeling to say the least. I survived and we won the game."

Long time professor at EC, Ovid Vickers, who taught at the school for 40 years, recalls attending numerous Warrior-Lion football games and is a virtual encyclopedia of information about the rivalry. Vickers remembers one game at Scooba in the '60s when the two teams got into a major brawl, which was not unusual then or now. According to Vickers, "An EC faculty member was at the game at Scooba cheering on the Warriors the night the fight took place. At a critical point in the game, something happened that upset the EC fans and the faculty member, who stood up in the bleachers directly behind the EC players and yelled where everyone could plainly hear, 'Double-up, double-up and fight.' All hell broke loose. The two teams raced toward each other colliding at mid-field and started fighting. Where they came from I do not know, but all of a sudden some of the players on both sides were using metal folding chairs as weapons to beat the other over their heads. The melee' on the field intensified, which seemed to have occurred when the metal folding chairs were introduced into the ruckus. EC's coach attempted to subdue the angry mob. However, several of his players grabbed him and pulled him out of the danger zone for fear he would get injured. The EC players restrained their head coach even as he tried valiantly to return to the battle. You could hear the EC coach screaming at his players to release him from his bondage along with questioning the genetic origin of his protectors. After what seemed like an eternity, the two teams were finally separated by local law enforcement officials and the Highway Patrol. Fortunately, the game resumed without further incident except for the controlled combat on the football field."

UNFORGETTABLE MOMENT 1928 TO PRESENT

WARRIORS VS LIONS

Every game played between East Central and East Mississippi is an unforgettable moment. The two schools do not care for one another, primarily due to their close proximity. The game between the Warriors and Lions is a bona fide, down home rivalry. Fans can count on a hard fought game played to the end every time the two teams clash. Often things get out of hand and all hell breaks loose.

Professor Vickers recalls another incident involving, not football players, but mascots of the two rivals, "Apparently, EC's Warrior Chief and the Lion mascot of Scooba were exchanging pleasantries before the game started. No one knows exactly what triggered the event but the verbal exchange reached a tipping point. All of a sudden the Warrior Chief charged the Lion. The impact not only knocked the Lion to the ground but, in the process, the most shameful of mascot atrocities occurred, the Lion's head came off. To add insult to injury, the person inside the Lion costume sustained three cracked ribs. As it turned out, after a full investigation by school officials and the ASPCA, the Warrior Chief was head of EC's Baptist Student Union."

Before he became East Central's seventh president, Phil Sutphin recalls yet another Scooba-EC "situation" which occurred toward the end of a game he was attending many years ago, "Scooba had the ball deep in Warrior territory with time running down on the clock and EC clinging to a three point lead. It was first and goal for Scooba inside the EC ten yard line. The first play was stopped for no gain by the Warrior defense. As the clock was ticking down and no time outs remaining, the Scooba quarterback quickly got his team back to the line of scrimmage and, after receiving the snap, spiked the ball to stop the clock. However, in doing so he spiked it behind him not in front. Instead of an incomplete pass the Scooba quarterback had fumbled and in the process an EC player fell on the ball recovering the fumble. As things were being sorted out on the field the Scooba coaches were protesting the call, which could determine the outcome of the game. The appeals of the Lions' coaches were denied and EC was awarded possession of the ball with just seconds remaining on the clock."

Sutphin continues, "When the Warriors' offense lined up right before the ball was snapped, a Scooba player kicked it into the end zone. No one noticed the referees' flags because all the players on the field were engaged in World War III. Instantly, both benches emptied, spilling onto the field, and joined in the brawl. It wasn't until the Decatur police drove their squad cars on the field and into the raging battle that they were able to restore order with the help of the campus police."

Even the current EC band director, Tom Carson (1973), recalls an incident with Scooba while he was a student in Decatur. According to Carson, "It was the week of the big game against Scooba which was to be played at their stadium. Some of my fellow band members and I were at the band hall after practice the evening before the game. Suddenly, a group of three or four guys walked into the band hall and said, 'Hi, how are y'all doing?' One of the guys remarked, 'We need to pick up the bass drum to get it repaired before tomorrow night.' We didn't think anything of it. The next day, I learned that EC's bass drum had been stolen by the Scooba operatives."

The night of the game at Scooba, EC's band was performing without its big bass drum. At some point during the pre-game activities someone in EC's band spotted their big bass drum sitting on the roof of a three story men's dormitory surrounded by a group of Scooba students. When several members of EC's band pointed to the location of the drum, trying to get their band director's attention, a Scooba student lifted the EC drum and threw it off the roof sending it crashing to the ground. As the drum was in its free fall to the ground there were bloodcurdling yells from the Scooba students mocking the EC Warriors' war chant.

Ricky Harrison (1976-77) remembers growing up and hearing his dad talk to his friends about how tough Juco football was. He recalls going to the barber in Decatur and seeing the Warriors' football schedule hanging on the wall in the shop year after year. Harrison was intrigued with the schools'

mascots and the names of the towns where EC opponents were located. One of EC's opponents that was talked about, and cursed, the most was in a town with a funny name. He also heard stories of a famous coach who was said to be crazy and who lived in the same town with the funny name. As Harrison was growing up he became eager to be a part of the excitement of Warrior football. He looked forward to the day when he could wear an EC uniform and go to all those towns he had seen on the Warriors' schedule in the barber shop in Decatur. His time finally came in September 1976.

East Central's number 12, Ricky Harrison, made his first appearance as a Warrior in a stadium located in that town with the funny name and against that team with the crazy former head coach who was now legendary. Unfortunately for him the team the Warriors were playing wanted to tear his number 12 jersey apart with him in it. Harrison found himself quarterbacking the Warriors against their most hated rival, the East Mississippi Lions. Welcome to Scooba!

During Harrison's first visit to Scooba, he was not on the field when it happened late in the third quarter. A Warrior defensive back had just picked off a Scooba pass and returned it down the EC sideline before getting pushed out of bounds. When the EC player turned to hand the football to the official he

got leveled by a Lion player clearly after the play was over. While the events were unfolding on the EC sideline, Harrison and the offense were sitting on the bench behind the action. Well, as expected, the Warriors retaliated and a fight erupted.

Harrison recalls two things about the melee', "I noticed the Scooba players, who were wearing their red jerseys that day, swarming across the field toward our sideline. I thought this must have been what it looked like when the British Redcoats charged General Washington during the Revolutionary War."

The second thing Harrison recalls was "Coach Coates grabbing me and Bill Barnett by our face masks and pulling us away from the fight saying, 'Y'all are my only two quarterbacks, you stay right here. I can't afford for either of you to get hurt.' I must admit I was somewhat relieved."

Harrison remembers another Scooba-EC game played at Decatur in the '60s that he attended as a spectator. "Back in the '60s the Warrior Chief rode a painted horse around the field during the games. Apparently the Warrior Chief got too close to Scooba's sidelines and they took offense. All of a sudden the Scooba players were pulling the Warrior Chief off his horse and roughing him up. One second he was riding the horse, then the next second, the horse was riderless and the Warrior chief was on the ground surrounded by Scooba players. It was scary."

Of course, the rivalry against East Mississippi hasn't produced all of EC's big games over the years. Boe Davis (1954-55) remembers the 1955 game against Hinds Junior College lead by their big bruising fullback, Jim Taylor. Taylor later become an All-American at LSU and All-Pro with the Green Bay Packers. With EC leading Hinds 13-7 late in the game and facing a fourth and three situation deep in their own territory, Coach Clayton Blount decided not to punt and gamble that the Warriors could maintain possession of the ball and run out the clock and preserve the upset victory.

Davis recalls the situation, "Charlie Hope was the quarterback and he looked over at Coach Blount on the sideline to find out what to do. Coach Blount really didn't say anything, but just turned his back to us, and running back James Gordon said, 'Let's just run the darn ball,' and we did. Gordon carried the pigskin and with a lot of help from the linemen we made the first down and eventually won the game. Coach Blount commented years later that the win over Hinds was the greatest win of his coaching career."

Jimmy Rea (1956-57) recalls the first highlight of his football career at EC was just being a member of the team, "Heck, I even loved practice as much as being in a game."

The highlight of Mark Killens (1978-79) career at EC was the Warriors upset win over the Jones Bobcats who came to Decatur in 1978 sporting a 9-0 record. Sportswriter Austin Bishop of the *Meridian Star* began his account of the stunning victory as follows:

"We interrupt this program to bring you this important message. World War III has broken out, the dollar is now only worth 17 cents and Jones Junior College has lost a football game. The last one is hard to believe, but it is the only one that is true. EC defeated the third-ranked Bobcats 21-16 at Warrior Field."

Having taught English and a variety of other courses for over four decades, Professor Vickers has the insight to put it all in perspective. Looking back to when he first arrived in Decatur in 1955 all the way to

UNFORGETTABLE MOMENT
1939 WARRIOR TEAM

1939 STATE FOOTBALL CHAMPIONS:

Although the East Central Warriors have experienced numerous successful seasons over the past 75 years, only the 1939 team can claim a state championship. Coached by the legendary Polie Sullivan, East Central rolled to a perfect 10-0 record in 1939, outscoring opponents 243-25 in the process.

Lamar Blount of Decatur was a standout member of the championship squad and is recognized as the first East Central athlete to receive All-American honors.

The Warriors clinched the state title by defeating Scooba in the season finale. East Central beat "little LSU" of Monroe, Louisiana, for the Southeast Regional Championship.

today, he has seen it all. Professor Vickers has lived the time line, making his comments highly instructive. "The game was much rougher in the earlier days than it is today. The game became more controlled starting in the '80s. The equipment worn by today's players is far superior to the gear worn by the players in the old days. Back then it was metal cleats and leather helmets without face masks. To put it in context, the most popular music when I first came to EC was jazz and big band. Well, let me just say, today 'Tiny Bubbles in the Wine' is not on the students Top 40 playlist."

Vickers continues, "Making the team was more competitive in the early days than it is today. In order for many of the kids in the '40s and '50s to afford college the only way was to get an athletic scholarship of some kind. Otherwise, it was off to work they would go. A football scholarship was a way to get an education so players were willing to endure a great deal to make the team. There was no quitting if you were fortunate enough to make it."

Interestingly, there is one thing that has not changed during the 40 years Professor Vickers was at EC. "The community has always been very supportive of the football team. When I first started teaching it was just assumed that you were interested in football. It was, and still is, a big part of the culture of this community," comments Vickers.

EC alum Malcolm Phillips (1946-48), a standout offensive and defensive end, began his coaching career in 1950 after graduating from Mississippi State University. It was at Humes High School in Memphis, Tennessee that Phillips had the opportunity to coach two unforgettable individuals; one who evolved from being the "meanest person who ever lived" to a respected evangelist, and the other aspiring athlete who later became an international superstar.

Phillips explains, "One of my former students, John 'Bull' Bramlett, was really the meanest person I have ever known. Later he became a Christian and one of the finest people I've known. He wrote a book titled *Taming of the Bull* and it is quite fascinating to read how he became the person he is today."

The other former player was also a character Phillips would never forget. Phillips recalls, "A shy, poor kid by the name of Elvis Presley went out for spring training his junior year at Humes. I remember watching this scrawny kid try to hit the blocking sled and I asked one of my assistants who he was. 'That's Presley, Coach,' he answered. Another time it was a very cold day and I told the players to keep their helmets on at all times so they would not get sick. Everyone kept his helmet on except Presley, who took it off repeatedly to slick his hair back."

Phillips says, "Presley lasted about 10 days and had to quit because he needed to make money. I still laugh when I remember my reaction to the first time I heard Presley perform on stage. There was a talent show at the school one night and I was working the concession area. When Presley got on stage and started singing, he quickly attracted a large crowd. I can still recall what I said when I heard him sing, I commented to the people around me that I didn't know what he was doing, but I was sure it would never catch on. Boy, was I wrong."

★   ★   ★   ★   ★

"I arrived in Meridian by bus and one of the coaches picked me up to take me to Decatur. We stopped at a drug store to get a cup of coffee and something to eat. When I asked the waitress in my Brooklyn accent for a piece of apple pie, she had no idea what I was saying. Although we experienced a little communication problem, it did not take long for the people in Decatur to get used to me and for me to get used to them. I really enjoyed myself at EC," recalls Sam Rutigliano (1950-51).

The obvious question is, why did a 17 year old from New York City come to Decatur, Mississippi to attend college and play sports? Rutigliano explains, "During my junior year at Erasmus High School, which was 1949, we won the city championship in football. But my high school career was stopped cold in 1950 because the New York City coaches went on strike. I was so upset that football had been taken away from me that I quit school and got a job delivering telegrams for RCA in the city. A while later, a recruiter from the University of Tennessee came to see me. He had read about our city championship and the coaches' strike. He told me that the University of Tennessee would pay all the costs of sending me to East Central Junior College in Decatur, Mississippi where I could finish high school and play football too. I gladly accepted the offer to go to Mississippi and then on to Tennessee."

Rutigliano says, "I was viewed somewhat as a curiosity since I was from New York City. I was called 'Yankee' all the time, probably because most people did not know how to pronounce my name. Nevertheless, I made many lasting friends in Mississippi."

Attending church each Sunday was a challenge for Rutigliano since he was Catholic and there were few Catholic churches in Mississippi in the '50s.

"I had to hitchhike 40 miles to Meridian to attend church. What a difference between Decatur and New York City. You can find a Catholic church about every six or eight blocks in New York City. I had to get up two or three hours earlier than usual on Sunday morning so I could get to Mass on time," recalls Rutigliano.

In addition to the culture shock, Rutigliano remembers the heat and humidity, which were sometimes unbearable. He says, "I remember walking into the locker room one day following a really tough practice and seeing a big wooden barrel full of water not far from the showers. Well, I was so hot and tired I literally sat in the barrel of water and never made it to the showers."

After his time at EC, Rutigliano attended the University of Tennessee where he played for the legendary General Robert R. Neyland. Upon graduation from college he coached in New York City high schools until he accepted his first job at the college level, the University of Connecticut. From UConn he went on to coach at the University of Maryland and later began his coaching career in the National Football League. Rutigliano had stints with Denver, New England, New York Jets, and New Orleans. He realized his lifelong dream in 1978 when he became the head coach of the Cleveland Browns. While he was at Cleveland, Rutigliano was twice named AFC Coach of the Year and was selected NFL Coach of the Year in 1980 after leading the Browns to an 11-5 record and the AFC Central Division title.

The strange twists and turns of life whereby one EC alumnus turns out to be the only football coach Elvis Presley ever had, while another former Warrior, from of all places Brooklyn, New York, ends up being one of the NFL's all time greatest coaches. Both Phillips and Rutigliano were proud members of that tribe of Warriors way down south in Decatur, Mississippi and both still fondly recall the beat of the war drums.

EAST CENTRAL	7
MIDDLE GEORGIA COLLEGE	6

Brunswick, GA, December 1996:

Mack Pittman's seven-yard touchdown run followed by Shaun Walker's PAT late in first half action lifted East Central Community College to a 7-6 win over Middle Georgia College in the second annual Huddle House Golden Isles Bowl Classic in Brunswick, Georgia. The bowl matchup was billed as the "Battle of Warriors" as each team has the same mascot.

Both teams had opportunities to score in the second half. EC's Walker barely missed a 32-yard field goal late in the third quarter, and Middle Georgia's Chris Mullis' 37-yard effort with 4:16 left in the game was also not successful.

East Central then took possession on its 20 yard line and proceeded to drive almost the length of the field behind runs by Pittman and fullback Steve Bradford, a product of Scott Central High School. Instead of scoring, East Central chose to run out the clock from the Middle Georgia four-yard line.

East Central completed the season with a 10-1 mark compared to Middle Georgia's 8-4 record.

EAST CENTRAL'S HEAD COACH ROSTER

Dick Baxter 1923-1932

Pat Wilson 1933-1938

Polie Sullivan 1939-1942

*1943-1944

Frank Cross 1945

Carrol Shows 1946

M.L. Vines 1947

Hillery Horne 1948-1950

John Grace 1951-1953

Billy Lindsley 1954

Clayton Blount 1955-1957

Bobby Oswalt 1958-1961

Tommy Guthrie 1962-1964

Dan Chatwood 1965-1966

Ken Pouncey 1967-1981

A.J. Kilpatrick 1982-1991

Reese Bridgeman 1992-1994

Willie Coats 1995-1997

Terry Underwood 1998-2007

Steve Cheatham 2008-2009

Brian Anderson 2009 to present

Brian Anderson

* No football due to World War II

EAST CENTRAL'S RECRUITING DISTRICT

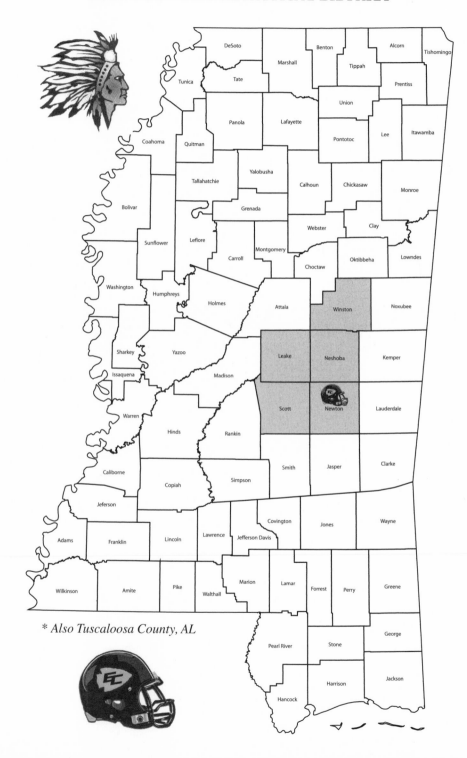

Also Tuscaloosa County, AL

EAST CENTRAL'S DISTRICT HIGH SCHOOLS

All Saints Academy
Carthage Christian
Choctaw Central
Forest
Grace Christian
Lake
Leake Academy
Leake Central
Leake County
Louisville
Morton
Nanih Waiya
Neshoba Central
Newton
Newton Central
Noxapater
Philadelphia
Pine Grove Academy
Scott Central
Sebastopol
Union
Winston Academy
* Also Tuscaloosa County, AL

EAST CENTRAL COMMUNITY COLLEGE
VS.
HINDS COMMUNITY COLLEGE

WARRIOR

WARRIOR
FOOTBALL

2:00 P.M. • OCTOBER 2, 2010 • BAILEY STADIUM

EAST MISSISSIPPI COMMUNITY COLLEGE
Scooba, Mississippi • Founded 1927 • Enrollment 5,000
Red, White & Black • Lions
Sullivan-Windham Stadium • Capacity 5,000
Marching Band: Mighty Lion Band

Chapter

6

//

A BLACK LEATHER HELMET

Football helmets are fascinating objects. An astute observer can look beyond the hard surface to something more meaningful than the protective qualities of a helmet. Take for instance the colors and the decals that decorate a player's helmet. To most observers these are nothing more than accessories that complete the player's uniform. But look deeper, don't focus on what is on the surface of the helmet, instead concentrate on what the colors and decals represent. Football helmets can be quite symbolic. Behind the colors and decals you can discover the personality of a school.

Consider some examples. While most college football teams tend to change the look of their uniforms from season to season, or from coach to coach, a small number of teams remain outfitted in the same uniforms year after year. Some even stay in the same uniform for decades. Regardless of the exciting new look of the trendy Oregon Ducks, most of the "evergreen" teams such as Penn State, Notre Dame, Alabama, Michigan, Nebraska, Texas and Florida State, to name a few, choose not to enter the fashion race. And particularly the helmets of these evergreen teams have remained the same for quite some time.

It appears that the evergreen programs have found a sense of comfort and satisfaction in their consistent appearance. The no frills white head gear with a dark blue stripe of Joe Paterno's Nittany Lions sums up his conservative, no-nonsense coaching style of the Penn State program for the past 45 years. The instantly recognizable golden helmet of the Fighting Irish symbolizes the famous golden dome of the administration building on the Notre Dame campus. Alabama and Michigan's helmets are instantly recognizable and broadcast the tradition of these two universities' storied football programs. All the helmets of the evergreen college teams have become iconic football symbols recognizable worldwide and whose trademarks have become priceless.

There is yet another school that possesses one of these iconic symbols which is associated with its football helmet--a helmet made famous by a legendary coach in the '50s and '60s. The color of the helmet is black. The helmet is made of leather, and is worn without a face mask. Emblazoned on the front of the helmet in white is a symbol that tells the story of their legendary coach and expresses the personality of the school and of its community. That symbol--a skull and crossbones; the coach--Bull Cyclone Sullivan; and his team--the Lions of Scooba, Mississippi.

He arrived on the East Mississippi Junior College campus in Scooba, Mississippi the summer of 1949. Bob Sullivan, all 6 feet 4 inches and 250 pounds of him, was traveling across the deep south in search of football players for his team up in the Pacific northwest--the University of Oregon Ducks.

Sullivan had migrated from his home in Aliceville, Alabama to Jackson, Tennessee to attend school and play football at Union College. However, his college days were interrupted by World War II. Sullivan joined the Marine Corps and saw combat duty in the South Pacific. After the war he returned to Union College and completed his degree requirements. Since the college had suspended its football team during the war years Sullivan was recruited by the University of Nevada at Reno to play out his remaining two years of eligibility. It was at Reno that he met "Whistlin Jim" Aiken, the head coach of the Wolf Pack. After his playing days at Reno, Sullivan followed Coach Aiken to the University of Oregon as an assistant when Aiken was named head coach. It was a year later that Sullivan found himself "duck hunting" on the Scooba campus the summer of 1949.

During his visit to Scooba, Sullivan met Cruce Stark, the President of East Mississippi. The President took a liking to Sullivan and offered him the head football coaching position at the college. Toward the end of the year Sullivan contacted President Stark and accepted the job as the Lions' head football coach. Stark didn't down play the team's winless season and the massive exodus of coaches and players. Nonetheless, in early 1950 Sullivan and his family were moving into the first floor apartment in the athletic dorm known as "the Alamo."

UNFORGETTABLE MOMENT NOVEMBER - 1964

THE INFAMOUS JONES GAME:

Played November 7, 1964 at Scooba, the undefeated Lions were beaten by arch-rival Jones County Junior College 32-13 to spoil East Mississippi's trip to the Junior Rose Bowl and a shot at the National Championship. During the game Scooba's All-American quarterback, Bill Buckner, was sent to the hospital with a severly broken jaw. Public opinion seemed to favor the notion that the incident on the field involving Buckner's injury was an intentional act of violence to get him out of the game. The teams discontinued playing each other for ten years before resuming play.

Along with finding players for his first season at Scooba, Sullivan also had to find games. True to form his first call was to defending national champion, Little Rock Junior College (Arkansas). As it turned out, the Little Rock team was in need of a warm-up game to start the 1950 season. Consequently, the national champion Little Rock team was eager to accommodate Sullivan's death wish. From the moment Little Rock agreed to play the game, Sullivan started working every psychological angle available. Within a week of announcing the game against the Little Rock team, Sullivan's players, the EMJC campus and all of Kemper County were in a frenzy. Little did Sullivan know at the time that his colorful legacy had begun.

Everybody was talking about the Lions' new head coach, who was either proclaimed by the fans as fearless or senseless. No one was sure just yet which one he was. Did he really think poor little winless Scooba Tech, as the school was sometimes called by its rivals, could compete with the elite of the junior college world? Juco football aficionados across the country thought this was just a publicity stunt by the new, unknown head coach of a backwater school in Mississippi. The big question throughout the country was not whether Little Rock would win, but whether the slaughter of the innocent

would take longer than one quarter of play. Little did the Juco football world realize that the legend of Bull Cyclone Sullivan was about to begin at the expense of the unsuspecting national champion Little Rock team. Back in Scooba, EMJC players and fans were about to find out that their new head coach was scared of absolutely no one, and he was about to prove it.

After a series of newspaper articles appeared in the Little Rock papers quoting the Little Rock coach that the upcoming game with EMJC was just a "tune-up" game for his team, Coach Sullivan unleashed his motivational skills. His psychological warfare was aimed directly at every man, woman and child in Kemper County. Suddenly, like a quickly developing thunderstorm fueled by the intense heat and humidity of a July afternoon in the South, the Little Rock game was transformed into an approaching storm with the potential to destroy everything in its path.

LION'S TRIVIA:

Scooba Cheer: Beat that drum, ring that bell, ECJC go to hell.

What began as Sullivan's inaugural game as the Lions' new head coach had now become the last stand for everyone associated with EMJC. It was no longer the Lions versus Little Rock JC. No! It was the evil, defending national champion team versus every living creature who was affiliated in any way with EMJC, together with the entire state of Mississippi, and every member of the free world (excluding of course the state of Arkansas) in a Holy War! The trip to War Memorial Stadium no longer had anything to do with football. It was now all out war, Bull Cyclone Sullivan style.

Finally, the long anticipated game between the small, no-name Mississippi school and the defending national powerhouse Little Rock team arrived. Back in Scooba, a crowd of people gathered at the Alamo where a radio capable of picking up the game all the way from Little Rock was plugged in and the volume turned up to its limit awaiting the broadcast. As the game unfolded, townspeople would come and go from the Alamo with the latest reports of what was taking place on the field at War Memorial Stadium. The final outcome was not what the football experts had predicted. The EMJC

Lions defeated the heavily favored Trojans by a score of 34-14. The football world was in shock and the legend of Bull Cyclone Sullivan was sweeping the country like a tsunami.

To further fuel the Sullivan legacy, over the years numerous stories circulated about his relationship with Paul "Bear" Bryant, the famous coach of the Alabama Crimson Tide. There is no dispute the two men frequently went fishing together at a location between Scooba and Tuscaloosa, Alabama. The same can be said for their meetings at the Smoke Shop in Columbus, Mississippi where they swapped stories of how to terrorize college football players.

Other stories about Bull and the Bear are more difficult to document. However, if frequency of hearing these stories counts toward making them credible, then they most certainly qualify as true. For instance, it is told by many that when Coach Bryant was disgusted with his Crimson Tide players, he threatened to put them on a bus to Scooba and let Bull Sullivan teach them about toughness.

UNFORGETTABLE MOMENT
SEPTEMBER - 1950

EMJC STUNS LITTLE ROCK (ARKANSAS)

The Lions from East Mississippi Junior College stunned the defending National Champion Little Rock Trojans 34-14 in both team's season opener. The large crowd at War Memorial Stadium in Little Rock, Arkansas anticipated a tune-up game for the Trojans. Instead the Scooba team, under first year head coach Bull Cyclone Sullivan, turned the evening into a nightmare for the defending national champions.

What is undisputed is that the two men were friends, both became coaching legends in their own right, and both left an indelible mark on their players and the game of football.

One of the most frequently recounted stories in the vast collection of Sullivan lore involves his teams scrimmages in the pond. When Sullivan sensed that his team was losing its focus during practice, if the offensive unit started getting careless, or when the defense started missing tackles, out came the roaring command, "To the pond!" Those three words set into motion a procession of gridiron warriors running across the pasture and through the broom straw to continue practice in the water of a small pond.

Depending on Sullivan's level of frustration with the offensive or defensive units, the rules of the scrimmage were adjusted accordingly. If the defensive unit caused his ire, the ball was placed right on the edge of the water. The only defensive personnel positioned on land were the down linemen, while the remainder of the unit took their positions knee deep in water.

If Sullivan wanted to chastise the offensive unit, the ball was placed ten yards from the edge of the water, allowing the defensive team to occupy dry land. No matter which version of the drill was in play, the defensive players always had their backs to the pond, while the offensive players always had the advantage of running downhill toward the water. Sullivan never denied he favored his offensive unit--especially quarterbacks--over the defensive unit.

The object of the drill was quite simple. The offense was supposed to drive the defensive unit into the water and preferably drown them. The only way the defensive bunch could avoid drowning was to hold their ground and not give up an inch.

If the offense got the upper hand during those titanic struggles it was not uncommon to see linebackers and safeties up to their chests in water. As the scrimmage moved deeper into the pond, the players' uniforms and equipment became waterlogged and heavy. Each play created more fatigue. However, the biggest danger was the pile ups at the end of the play. A player dared not get trapped on the bottom of a pile.

Not only did players have to be alert during scrimmages to avoid becoming trapped in the murky water of Sullivan's pond, they also had to be aware of another danger--snakes. A number of water moccasins inhabited the area around the practice mud hole. If the team lost its focus on the practice field Sullivan would not hesitate to relocate to the snake-infested water site for attitude adjustment therapy.

Sullivan was adept at knowing when to dial up just the right degree of pressure to keep his team focused, and he constantly changed his approach to keep them off balance. They never knew what he might do next. As if being driven into snake-infested waters wasn't enough, Sullivan added another motivational dimension to the scrimmages in the pond--alligators.

Sullivan brought home a few baby alligators from a family vacation in Florida one summer and relocated them to the pond. Apparently, the baby alligators found the climate and other amenities of the area conducive to their growth....and reproduction. It wasn't long before Sullivan's Pond featured yet another element of motivation for the players. Lurking behind the defensive players on the edge of the pond was not only snake-infested water, but a half dozen alligator spectators as well. How exciting this must have been for all the players fortunate enough to be involved in the scrimmage!

While some doubt the credibility of the seemingly outlandish tales about the scrimmages in Sullivan's Pond, there are numerous eye witnesses to confirm that the events did take place. John Kenneth Briggs, Jr. (1962-64) testifies, "I watched 22 men scrimmage in the pond with my own eyes."

Long after other teams had turned in their old leather helmets for the state-of-the-art modern plastic ones with face masks, Coach Sullivan kept his team in no face mask leather headgear.

The skull and crossbones symbol debuted on the Scooba black leather helmets in 1959. Coach Sullivan assigned the important duty of painting the insignia on the helmets to his most trusted assistant, his wife Virginia. Sullivan's oldest daughter, Bobbie, is credited with finding the design that was painted on each helmet. According to Bobbie, "Mother had all these helmets to paint and she couldn't find a skull and crossbones pattern anywhere. I told her to look at the Red Devil Lye package; maybe it had the skull and crossbones on it. Well, it did. That's where the design came from--Red Devil Lye." Bobbie remembers her daddy saying, "Just think how the other team is gonna feel when they see that skull and crossbones on the helmets with no face masks."

No doubt, one of the reasons Sullivan used the Red Devil Lye moniker and the black leather helmet without face masks was to gain a psychological advantage over his opponents. In addition, Sullivan strongly believed that the leather helmets worn by his Scooba players were safer than the modern plastic helmets with face masks. He was convinced that wearing a helmet without a face mask forced a player to learn to protect himself when he tackled. The face mask gave a player a false sense of security thereby leading to many neck injuries.

Scooba's black leather helmets with the now famous skull and crossbones insignia on the front symbolized the discipline and toughness required of players during the Sullivan era. One of Sullivan's sons, Little Vic, remembers "When Scooba played in the Hospitality Bowl in 1963 against

Tyler, Texas, the Texas players admitted at the banquet following the game that they were terrified by those black leather helmets. At first they thought they were just practice helmets. When they saw the skull and crossbones on the helmet with no face masks, it really scared them."

Scooba's black leather helmet might have gone unnoticed outside of Juco football circles except for an article in *Sports Illustrated* in 1984. The title of the cover article in the April 30th edition of *SI* was "The Toughest Coach There Ever Was." The article was written by renowned sports writer Frank Deford and was an amazing 18 pages in length. Today, the Deford article remains one of the longest (if not the longest) articles ever to appear in the world famous magazine. The article was about the "Backwoods Bear," the coach at a small college in east Mississippi in a town named Scooba. That coach was Bull Cyclone Sullivan, and on the front cover of the April 30th, 1984 issue of *SI* was the black leather helmet of the EMJC Lions with the skull and crossbones directly on the front for the entire world to see. Yes, football helmets are fascinating objects.

Today, safety regulations prohibit the Lions from wearing the iconic leather helmets without face masks. However, on special occasions the Scooba players sport a flat black modern Riddell helmet with a distinctive skull and crossbones decal on each side. Bull Cyclone Sullivan would be proud.

EPIC G★MES

EAST MISSISSIPPI	75
MISSISSIPPI GULF COAST	71

Scooba, MS, 2009:

In a contest featuring 146 total points and 1,219 yards of combined total offense, the No.7 East Mississippi Lions dethroned two-time defending state champions and No.3 ranked Mississippi Gulf Coast Bulldogs in a wild 75-71 shootout to claim the 2009 MACJC State Football Championship.

Head coach Buddy Stephens' EMCC squad claimed the school's first ever state football title and tied an all time school standard with its 10th victory of the season.

With the score tied at 54-54 heading into the final period, the Lions and Bulldogs traded scores to keep the game deadlocked until midway through the fourth quarter. After Gulf Coast hit a 29-yard field goal at the 6:49 mark, EMCC struck from 11-yards to take the lead at 68-64.

EMCC's lead would not last long. With 2:48 remaining the Bulldogs scored on an 18-yard pass play to retake the lead 71-68. The Lion tandem of Randall Mackey and Lance Lewis hooked up for the would be winning touchdown with their fourth scoring connection of the game with only 1:38 left on the clock.

The Lion's seventh straight victory of the season, and their first state title, was preserved by sophomore free safety Anthony Hines with a game saving interception in the end zone.

EAST MISSISSIPPI'S HEAD COACH ROSTER

Johnny F. Almond 1929-1931

Stennis "Judge" Little 1932-1934

Ray Casper 1935-1936

Z.L. Sheriff Knight 1937-1940

W.F. Childres 1941-1942

*1943-1945

V.C. Boyd 1946-1948

Marcus Mapp 1949

Bob "Bull Cyclone" Sullivan

   1950-1952

Roy Knapp 1953-1955

Bob "Bull Cyclone" Sullivan

   1956-1968

Bull Cyclone Sullivan

A.J. Kilpatrick 1969-1970

Bill Buckner 1971-1974

Jackie Reese 1975

Randall Bradberry

   1976-1987

J.C. Arban 1988-1990

Danny Adams 1991

Tom Goode 1992-2003

Roger Carr 2004-2007

Buddy Stephens 2008 to present

Buddy Stephens

* *No football due to World War II*

EAST MISSISSIPPI'S RECRUITING DISTRICT

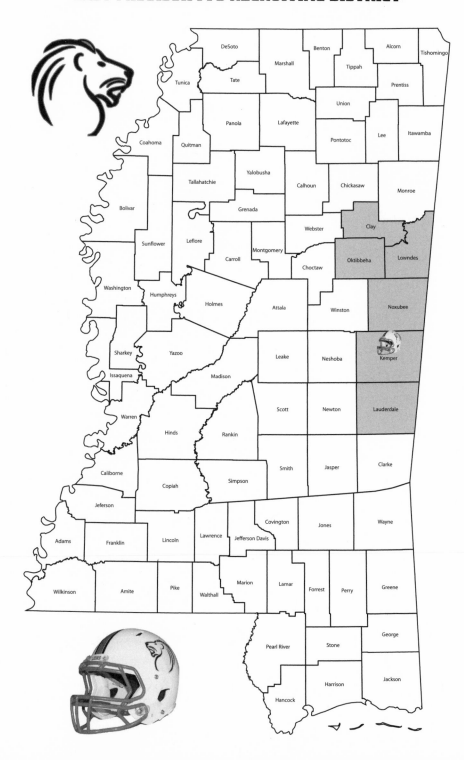

EAST MISSISSIPPI'S DISTRICT HIGH SCHOOLS

Hebron Christian School

Oak Hill Academy

West Point

Kemper Academy

Kemper County

Calvary Christian School

Clarkdale

Lamar School

Meridian

Northeast Lauderdale

Russell Christian Academy

Southeast Lauderdale

West Lauderdale

Caledonia

Columbus

Heritage Academy

Immanuel

New Hope

Victory Christian School

West Lowndes

Central Academy

Noxubee County

East Oktibbeha

Starkville Academy

Starkville

West Oktibbeha

Official Program

SCOOBA
JUNIOR COLLEGE
VS.
DECATUR
JUNIOR COLLEGE
★

Ray Stadium
Saturday, October 28, 1950

Sponsored By
MERIDIAN LIONS CLUB

COPIAH-LINCOLN COMMUNITY COLLEGE

Wesson, Mississippi • Founded 1928 • Enrollment 3,800

Blue & Gray • Wolfpack

H.L. "Hook" Stone Stadium • Capacity 5,000

Marching Band: Blue Wave Show Band

Chapter
7

//

THOSE WE HONOR

December 31, 1863:

The powerful canons of the advancing Union Army pounded the small east Mississippi town of Bankston until it was reduced to a burning pile of broken boards, bricks and an assortment of rubble. Somewhere in the smoldering debris were scraps of building materials that just hours earlier comprised the structures housing the large mercantile operations owned by Colonel J.M. Wesson.

Prior to the start of the war between the states (circa 1848), Colonel Wesson had moved his small textile operation from Columbus, Georgia to the foothills of Mississippi in Choctaw County. Colonel Wesson's new company, the Mississippi Manufacturing Company, developed multiple production divisions--a tannery, shoe manufacturing, a brickyard, wheat and grist mills, a sawmill and its largest operation, a giant textile mill. The Mississippi Manufacturing Company became such a successful enterprise that it earned Colonel Wesson the title "father of the cotton industry in Mississippi."

Unfortunately, Colonel Wesson and his Mississippi Manufacturing Company got caught in the confluence of events resulting in the collision between the northern and southern armies. Colonel Wesson's successful commercial operation was destroyed. Wesson watched as the structures housing his company were blown-up and burned to the ground in December of 1863.

Even as the Civil War continued to rage on, Colonel Wesson began prospecting for a new site to rebuild his former enterprise. His search lead him to an undeveloped ridge of wilderness in the pine forests near the Copiah and Lincoln County lines. The location was situated on the railroad route running from New Orleans to Chicago. The site selected by Colonel Wesson occupied a stretch of land between the Mississippi and Pearl Rivers. It was on this spot of land that Colonel Wesson chose to start over once the war ended.

A model of perseverance, Colonel Wesson launched into the rebuilding process with a blueprint for the success of his company and for

> **UNFORGETTABLE MOMENT**
> **NOVEMBER 1985**
>
> **WOLVES DEVOUR BULLDOGS, CAPTURE STATE CHAMPIONSHIP:**
>
> The Co-Lin Wolves defeated defending National Champions, Mississippi Gulf Coast, 24-23 to capture the Mississippi Junior College State Football Championship. Co-Lin last won the state title 47 years ago under legendary football coach, H.L. "Hook" Stone.

the new town that would bear his name. Over the next decade he navigated the post-war Mississippi Manufacturing Company and the town of Wesson through its humble beginnings to create a land of opportunity in the dense pine forests of southwest Mississippi.

Due to Colonel Wesson's visionary leadership, the little town of Wesson grew and prospered then boomed into an industrial giant not just in Mississippi, but in the world. While residents of Chicago and New York were still eating dinner by kerosene lamps during the late 1800s, the folks in the buzzing metropolis of Wesson were dining by electric light. The town became noted for its innovations in technology and Wesson became the home of the largest cotton textile mill in the world. During this boom period, Wesson was home to more millionaires than any other town in Mississippi.

Even when the Great Depression plagued the United States, the opportunities for the people in Wesson expanded. During the 1930s, Copiah-Lincoln Agricultural High School and Junior College offered a two year college education at an affordable price even to students during the depression era. From 1933 to 1971, the junior college expanded by adding five more counties to its district--Simpson, Franklin, Lawrence, Jefferson and Adams. As a consequence of the steady addition of these counties, Copiah-Lincoln Junior College grew at a consistent pace.

Today the college (now referred to as Copiah-Lincoln Community College, or Co-Lin) occupies 542 acres with more than 30 buildings dotting its Wesson campus. The college also maintains campuses in Natchez and Simpson County, Mississippi. Co-Lin provides a diverse selection of academic, career and technical programs to 3,800 students.

Since its founding in 1928, Co-Lin has served as the economic engine for the seven counties in its district, spawning opportunities for its students and their families. The college still provides educational benefits to its students, many of whom are the descendants of yesterday's students. And just like the town's founder, Colonel J.M. Wesson, Co-Lin continues to create opportunities for all those folks who are in search of their own new towns, enterprises and innovations.

There have been many changes in Wesson and at Co-Lin since the Colonel came to town 148 years ago, however, some things are destined to remain the same. While the opera house, movie theater, circus and medicine shows have been replaced by Skeet's Burgers and other area businesses, there is one thing that has remained in the community for quite some time. For three decades, serious discussions about serious topics have been debated at one of Wesson's oldest businesses, Furr's Service Station. One of the most frequently discussed topics and perhaps the most important topic to the locals, are the Wolves. Now don't be confused. The dense pine forests surrounding Wesson are not inhabited by packs of wild wolves. No, the locals are referring to the Co-Lin football team--the Wolfpack.

The Wolfpack football program began in 1927 under the guidance of H.L. "Hook" Stone. Coach Stone instantly put Co-Lin on the Juco football map winning eight state championships in the eleven years he coached the Wolves. During Coach Stone's stint at Co-Lin he served as the athletic director, head

football, basketball and baseball coach. The football stadium at Co-Lin was named in his honor in 1969.

Today the Wolfpack is led by veteran head football coach Glenn Davis, who took over the program in 2004. Between Coach Stone and Coach Davis, the Wolfpack teams have been guided by a number of outstanding coaches who have left their mark on Co-Lin's football program. Several of Coach Stone's successors such as James Sloan, Randall Bradberry and Phil Broome achieved success at Co-Lin during their respective tenures. Over the years,

Wolfpack teams have provided the college with championships, All-American players and exciting games. Several former Co-Lin players such as Victor Green, Tony Bryant, Randy Thomas, Cleveland Pinkney and Tim Dobbins, just to name a few, have gone on to play in the National Football League. Recent Co-Lin graduate Nick Fairley played a major part in Auburn University defeating the Oregon Ducks for the 2010 NCAA National Championship. Fairley was named the Most Outstanding Defensive Player of the game.

Fairley, the 6 foot 5, 298-pound junior received the Lombardi award as the nation's top collegiate lineman and was selected as the defensive player of the year on the Associated Press All-SEC Team, AP first Team All-American and was named to the Walter Camp All-American Team. Fairley was also a finalist for the Chuck Bednarirk award as the nation's best defensive player.

All coaches encounter situations with their players in helping them grow as athletes and students. Former Wolfpack head coach, Philip Broome recalls a player who came to Co-Lin from Franklin County. Actually, Lawrence was not recruited to play football at Co-Lin but ended up in Wesson by one of those twisted routes some recruits take before finally selecting where they will attend college. Unfortunately, Lawrence lived in a desperate situation and his dream was to get away from the poverty that surrounded him and to start a new life.

When Lawrence arrived at Co-Lin he was overwhelmed. He could not grasp that he would receive three meals everyday. At no time in his life was he ever provided with such a luxury. Co-Lin was like a fantasy world to Lawrence. In addition to the abundance of food, Lawrence was grateful for his living conditions in Lincoln Hall. To him, Stinkin' Lincoln was a five star hotel complete with running water, heat, air conditioning and best of all fellow guests. Lawrence had a family of teammates and for the first time in his life he had someone to watch over him. Coach Broome became the father figure Lawrence never had.

Lawrence was easy to like. He was so grateful for his new life and he enjoyed everything around him everyday. All the things that were taken for granted by most of the Co-Lin students, Lawrence viewed as blessings. Activities such as attending football practice, classes, weightlifting, going to the dining hall an incredible three times a day, getting to sleep in a bed every night and being able to take as many showers as he wanted were luxuries. Yes, life was great for Lawrence at Co-Lin!

WOLFPACK TRIVIA:

The old athletic dorm at Co-Lin was Lincoln Hall, an army barracks that had been converted into a dorm for male athletes. The dorm was unaffectionately referred to as "Stinkin Lincoln."

Lawrence's attitude of gratefulness was displayed by his eagerness to please others, especially Coach Broome. He went out of his way to help, doing anything he could for Coach. Lawrence enjoyed babysitting Coach's children, walking the family dog and even cooking for the Broome family on occasion. Oftentimes, Lawrence used Coach's truck to pick up the Broome children from school. It didn't take long for the Broome family and everyone else on the Co-Lin campus to love Lawrence as much as he loved being in Wesson, Mississippi.

During the off season, Lawrence trained like an olympian and became the key motivator on the team. He also assisted the coaches with recruiting. Lawrence became so effective in entertaining recruits that Coach Broome frequently gave him the keys to his truck so he could go to Jackson to greet recruits at the airport and drive them to campus for their official visits. Lawrence developed a reputation as a responsible guy who could be trusted. In a matter of months after his arrival on campus, Lawrence had made himself indispensable to Coach and the team. He was the go to guy.

One night while Coach was sleeping soundly in his apartment in the dorm, he was jolted awake at 2 a.m. by the ringing telephone. "Hello," answered Mrs. Broome in a semi-conscious state. "Yes, he's right here. Hold on and I'll get him." "Phillip, the Sheriff needs to speak to you about Lawrence."

UNFORGETTABLE MOMENT
DECEMBER 2006
CO-LIN STUNS GEORGIA MILITARY ACADEMY IN BOWL GAME

The Wolves' swarming defense handed the number eight ranked Georgia Military Academy their first shutout of the season limiting the Bulldogs to 48 yards total offense and just seven yards rushing. The 21-0 Co-Lin victory was the first shutout in the 12 year history of the Golden Isle Bowl.

After a brief exchange of words, Coach jumped out of bed, dressed quickly, grabbed the keys to his truck and said, "I'm heading to Crystal Springs and I'm not sure when I'll be back."

When Coach arrived at the Sheriff's office in Crystal Springs he was mad, actually bordering on furious. Of all people to get arrested, Lawrence! He was greeted by the Sheriff with a half smile and smirk. Coach forced out the dreaded question, "What did he do? Was he drinking?" "No," the Sheriff responded. "Did he get into a fight?" "No," said the Sheriff. "Did he rob somebody?" Again the Sheriff said, "No." "Oh my God, is it murder?" blurted Coach Broome. "No," the Sheriff said yet again.

With his anxiety rising over the uncertainty of the criminal act committed by Lawrence, Coach declared, "What in the hell did he do Sheriff?" The Sheriff finally revealed the charges against Lawrence but not without a long pause, "Umm, Coach, Lawrence was driving without a license." "What?" exploded Coach. "That's impossible. He has been driving for me all over town, going up to Jackson and running errands for me for over a year." The Sheriff responded calmly, "Coach, Lawrence doesn't have a drivers license. "Where is he? I want to see him right now. We need to get to the bottom of this," said Coach in a loud tone.

While the exchange between Coach Broome and the Sheriff was

taking place, Lawrence was in a cell in an adjacent room and could hear what was being said. Apparently he could sense things were not going well for him. On one hand, he had to answer to a judge for his criminal misconduct. But, on the other hand, he had to face Coach, and the prospect of that judgement day scared him the most.

Lawrence was straining to hear what was being said in the next room when all of a sudden it got quiet. It was then that Coach started retracing in his mind the scores of times he had sent Lawrence on errands for him, his family and the coaches--all in his truck. Coach imagined the consequences of what might have happened. His silence ended when he shouted loudly, "Sheriff, where is Lawrence? He's coming home with me."

Before the Sheriff could respond, he and Coach Broome could hear Lawrence pleading from the cell in the next room, "No, no, please Sheriff let me stay in jail. I want to stay behind bars. I'll do anything, just don't turn me over to Coach." Lawrence's antics amused the Sheriff so much  that he released him to Coach Broome who promptly escorted Lawrence to his truck for the ride back to Wesson.

The 20 mile ride back to the campus seemed like a cross-continental trip on a bicycle to Lawrence. As the minutes sluggishly passed by it seemed to Lawrence that time was frozen inside the silence of Coach's truck. Not one word was spoken until the two arrived back in Wesson. The silent scolding that coaches are so adept at delivering had taken its toll on Lawrence. Even though driving without a license was a misdemeanor punishable by a small fine it didn't matter to Lawrence. He had neglected to take care of his business while taking care of everyone else's business. He was truly ashamed of himself, but most of all, he was distraught because he had let Coach Broome down. Lawrence felt sick

Once in front of his dorm, Lawrence opened the door to get out of the truck when Coach finally broke the silence. "Grow up and take responsibility for your actions son," stated coach in a firm but calm voice. When Lawrence got out of the truck Coach said, "Lawrence, remember my two rules?" "Yes, Coach, I do," replied Lawrence. "Things are never as bad as they seem and get up and get going no matter what," said Lawrence. "That's right. Good night Lawrence," responded Coach Broome.

Another former head football coach for the Wolfpack and legendary Mississippi high school football coach, James Sloan, recalls both his playing and coaching experiences in the Mississippi Juco league. Sloan says, "The games were incredibly physical. Only the real tough, tough kids survived. People couldn't wait to see that mess. On a punt, don't you get caught standing there watching the ball roll dead. I'm telling you, now. Don't you break down around the football if the whistle hasn't blown. You had better be looking right and left. Don't worry about when the football's gonna stop rolling. They are just coming at you wide open."

From the rough style of play in the Juco league both coaches and players developed a certain toughness that leads to confidence in life. Coach Sloan recalls a discussion he had with one of his former players who served in the United States Marine Corps. According to Sloan, "He told me, 'Coach, the reason I made it was because I stepped over everybody who had gone down; and I kept on going until I got to the top of the hill. I just kept thinking, this is almost like two-a-day football practices.'"

The map of the Co-Lin campus looks like an ordinary map of a small city, community or college town. Any visitor to Wesson and the Co-Lin campus can quickly get his bearings and navigate around by locating the main streets, landmarks and key buildings on the map. Of course, street and building names provide a common language for visitors trying to find their way to a particular destination. The Co-Lin campus has the typical intersections of the main streets, the back routes and the short cuts well known to the locals. An astute observer of the street and building names will notice the continuity. There are no streets or buildings that have descriptive identification such as Peachtree Street or The Fine Arts Building. Every street and building on the Co-Lin campus bears the name of a person. The streets and buildings are all named for those the college honors, and each tells a unique story about the history of Co-Lin. Each street sign or building name is a story of an individual--a special person in the eyes of those who know about Co-Lin.

Take for example the street that circles Ellis Hall, Hillary Hallum Circle. It honors the man who first came to work at Co-Lin in the early 1930s. When Mr. Hallum began working at the college he walked to work each morning from Beauregard, some four miles away, leaving home at 4:00 a.m. to get to his job in the school cafeteria.

There is Hodges Lane named in memory of the Hodges family. F.B. and Frances Graham Hodges were instrumental in the founding of Copiah-Lincoln Agricultural High School. They moved to Wesson in 1913 from Jackson. All seven of their children attended Co-Lin.

McCarty Drive is named in memory of H.F. McCarty who was the owner of McCarty State Pride Poultry Farms, one of the largest poultry production operations in the United States. He graduated from Co-Lin in 1940 and was active in the Alumni Association until his death.

Roads such as Grover Smith Lane, J.C. Redd Drive, Shelby Pitts Drive, Ike Allen Circle, Lester R. Furr Drive, John Landress Circle and Oswalt Drive all memorialize names of contributors to pieces of Co-Lin's history.

Walter R. "Polie" Sullivan Baseball Stadium, Graydon L. Mullen Gym, the Sandifer Communications Building, the Stribling Associate Degree Nursing Building, Dan Watson Building and Dennis White Press Box at Sullivan Field...all names of people who in some way helped create the special place called Co-Lin.

EPIC G★MES

COPIAH-LINCOLN   18
NASSAU COUNTY N.Y.   17

Wesson, Mississippi, 1985:

The Wolves of Copiah-Lincoln hosted Nassau Community College of Garden City, New York in the East Bowl played November 30, 1985 in an afternoon contest.

Nassau located on Long Island was ranked number two in the nation by the National Junior College Athletic Association with a 10-0 record and winners of the Eastern Division title of the Coastal Athletic Conference. The conference is composed of schools in New England and other eastern states. Nassau has an enrollment of 23,245 students.

The Wolves, sporting a 9-3 record, entered the national title implication game as winners of the tough Mississippi Junior College Conference coming off an electrifying 24-23 win over perennial power Mississippi Gulf Coast.

A packed Stone Stadium crowd watched as the Wolves' "bend but never break" defense turned back Nassau's high-powered offense. Coach Ray Ishee of Co-Lin said, "We settled down and contained the highly touted Nassau quarterback, Anthony Meritt, in the second half with a number of interceptions. We were trying to mix it up on defense with either maximum rush or maximum coverage."

Meritt, the Lions' sensational quarterback who had passed for 1,425 yards in Nassau's 10-0 regular season, completed just 7 of 27 passes for only 83 yards against the Wolves' nimble defense. While the Nassau Lion's offensive line only allowed one quarterback sack, that play came on second down with less than two minutes left in the game when the Wolfpack nose guard, Willie Williams, tackled Meritt for a 14-yard loss at Nassau's 20.

The game produced a number of big plays keeping the 4,000 plus crowd on its feet throughout the afternoon. What eventually proved to be the winning points came on the conversion following the Wolves final touchdown when Co-Lin unveiled its Huddle play giving the Wolves the one point edge.

The 18-17 loss spoiled the Lions' undefeated season and a chance of winning the National Championship.

1966 Colettes

Coaches Louis B. Johnson and Marion Fortenberry (1941)

CO-LIN'S HEAD COACH ROSTER

Henry Lafayette "Hook" Stone 1928-1938

T.S. "Dick" Hitt 1939

Louis B. "Farmer" Johnson 1940-1944

Francis Marion Fortenberry 1945-1947

W.F. Bruce 1948-1949

Jack Nix 1950

J.W. Waites 1951-1952

John Gregory 1953

A.J. Mangum, Jr. 1954-1959

Wallace Hargon 1960-1962

Bob Ricketts 1963-1966

Jerry Taylor 1967-1969

Malcolm Nesmith 1970

C.B. Hawkins 1971-1978

James Sloan 1979-1984

Ray Ishee 1985-1989

Randall Bradberry 1990-1994

Phillip Broome 1995-2000

David Cross 2001

David Poinsett 2002-2003

Glenn Davis 2004-present

*H.L. "Hook"
Stone*

CO-LIN'S RECRUITING DISTRICT

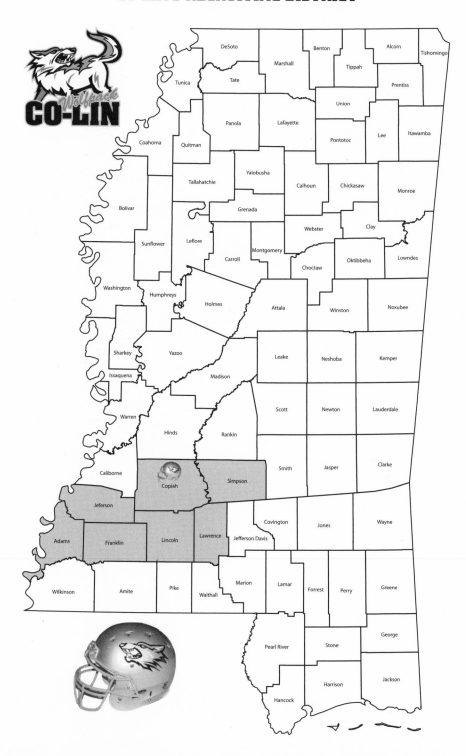

CO-LIN'S DISTRICT HIGH SCHOOLS

Wesson Attendance Center

Hazlehurst

Crystal Springs

Copiah Academy

Simpson County Academy

Mendenhall

Magee

Lawrence County

Franklin County

Natchez

Adams County Christian School

Cathedral

Trinity Episcopal School

Brookhaven

Enterprise

West Lincoln

Bogue Chitto

Loyd Star

Brookhaven Academy

Jefferson County

1985 EAST BOWL

COPIAH-LINCOLN
JUNIOR COLLEGE
WOLVES

VS.

NASSAU
COMMUNITY COLLEGE
LIONS

NOVEMBER 30, 1985   STONE STADIUM, WESSON, MS   PRICE $1.50

PEARL RIVER COMMUNITY COLLEGE

Poplarville, Mississippi • Founded 1921 • Enrollment 5,500

Maroon & Gold • Wildcats

Dobie Holden Stadium • Capacity 4,500

Marching Band: Spirit of the River

Chapter

8

//

THE BRONZE MAN

"**M**ississippi is on my mind. We are with you," said President George W. Bush as he addressed a gathering of about 250 elected state and local officials, including Mississippi Governor Haley Barbour, assembled on the campus of Pearl River Community College on Monday, September 5, 2005.

Just one week earlier, Hurricane Katrina devastated South Mississippi in a force not seen since Hurricane Camille hit the state in 1969. President Bush stated during his heartfelt remarks to those gathered in the cramped multi-purpose room in the Technology Center that the "people of Mississippi had shown courage...and had risked their lives to help one another."

Hurricane Katrina's winds that blew as high as 120 miles per hour across the Pearl River campus began just before dawn on Monday, August 29, 2005 and by the time they subsided it was after 3:00 p.m. Katrina left massive destruction in her wake.

By Monday evening all of South Mississippi began to feel the damage of Katrina on a broader scale. Power was out, communication lines disrupted, water systems compromised and roads washed away. The damage to buildings on the campus was extensive. M.R. White Coliseum suffered massive damage, Moody Hall's Auditorium, built in 1926 and the oldest classroom building among the state's fifteen junior colleges, was demolished. Two dormitories were close to destroyed and the school's vehicle maintenance shop virtually caved in. Every building on campus sustained some form of roof and water damage.

The bottom line financially--Pearl River suffered between $40-50 million in damages from Katrina. The president of Pearl River, Dr. William Lewis said, "This is worse than Hurricane Camille." According to Dr. John Grant in his article "PRCC Survives Another Storm", published in the special edition of the *Dixie Drawl*, September 2005, he writes, "August 29, 2005 will forever be remembered as the date of the worst natural disaster in American history, surpassing even the great flood of the Mississippi River in 1927, and Hurricane Andrew in South Florida in 1992."

Dr. Grant continues, "Everyone knew there would be hurricanes after Camille, and there were...Surely there could never be another so destructive as she. But, thirty-six years later, there was."

Immediately after the initial impact of the storm had passed, Pearl River officials began the tedious process of cleanup and rebuilding. Shockingly, power was restored to the campus within a week. There is a somewhat humorous story behind why the lights got turned on so soon following the storm.

President Lewis recalls the events, "Originally I had been informed by the power company it was going to take at least thirty days to get power restored to the campus. Of course, that posed major problems with ongoing repairs, possible loss of an entire school semester, just a total disruption to the entire community. Also, keep in mind this was late August, early September in Mississippi. Its hot, humid and everything is damp and waterlogged. Just a mess, a big mess."

President Lewis continues, "Well I got word that President Bush might be coming to Mississippi to inspect the damages and he *may* visit Pearl River. Then I got word the President *is* coming to Mississippi and to Pearl River. I knew it was for real when the secret service got involved in the planning. The Sunday before the President was scheduled to visit our campus, I was standing with some of our campus police at the only road coming in and out of campus that was open. It was starting to get dark and workers from the power company were starting to load up and leave after a long day of work. As the caravan of trucks, some of which were from as far away as New York, were leaving campus I was nodding to the men and saying 'I'll see you tomorrow.' I noticed as the long line of trucks got a hundred yards or so from where I was standing the convoy stopped. Well, I guess it was 10 to 15 minutes later and the trucks started turning around and headed back our way. Once back on campus the workers got out, unloaded their gear and went back to work. I thought to myself that sure is strange. Later, in the middle of the night the power to the campus came on. We had lights! What was expected to take at least thirty days was done in seven."

UNFORGETTABLE MOMENT
OCTOBER 1961

WILDCATS WIN, NAMED NATIONAL CHAMPIONS

The Pearl River Wildcats were voted the 1961 National Champions ending the season with a perfect 10-0 record. Pearl River dominated all of their opponents scoring 446 points while giving up only 47 the entire season.

"The day after President Bush had visited our campus I asked the supervisor of the workers for the power company, who was back doing some more repair work, why his crew stopped and then returned earlier in the week to work all night. He told me as they were leaving that day he received a call from the president of the power company who informed him that he had just received word that President Bush would be on campus the next day and the power had to be restored. Do what you have to do, but get it done. So that's what they did," recalls Lewis.

Several of Pearl River's sister schools throughout the state and even junior and community colleges in other states provided help in the wake of the Katrina disaster. Many of these schools sent skilled workers such as carpenters, electricians and plumbers to help restore campus facilities. Those schools that didn't provide direct aid offered President Lewis counsel and moral support. All the aid and assistance was much appreciated by the folks in Poplarville.

Tim Hatten, the Wildcats popular head football coach, offers another interesting prospective of the days following Katrina, "As bad as it was after the storm, there were some good things to come out of it. Our coaching staff and team really became tight during the 2005 season. Now we considered

ourselves pretty tight prior to the storm. The coaches' offices are located in a building next to the dorm where our players live. So we are all right there together. After Katrina everyone on campus was having to share space because of the shortage of operational offices. The football coaches' offices were moved inside the dorm where the players lived. Every day the players had to pass by the coaches because our desks were set up in the lobby of the dorm. Many of the players sat at the coaches' desks at night to study and use the computers. During this time we learned what it was like to literally live with your players. Because of this experience we did become closer as a team. It also showed the coaches how much more we could do to really connect with our players."

The following are excerpts from an open letter from President Lewis published in a special edition of the *Dixie Drawl* in September 2005. President Lewis' comments provide a clear insight into the thoughts of the folks of Poplarville and Pear River County immediately following the devastating storm. President Lewis writes:

Dear Friends,

Hurricane Katrina has reminded all of us that life is fragile and that we should never take tomorrow for granted. The aftermath of Katrina left us with so much devastation and yet so much to be thankful for.

Life has become more precious and the material things of our daily existence seem not to be quite as important. There seems to be a new humbleness in our people and a new resolve that the things of life may quickly melt away, but the spirit of goodness that abides within us will overcome the tragedies of life.

So it is with our institution....

The 2005-06 school year had begun with much promise. A record enrollment of over 4300 students had enrolled at the college. The largest marching band in our school's history and a football team that was ranked No. 1 in the country in the preseason polls were precursors to a fantastic school year. The year held so much promise and still does.

We are determined, and I am convinced, that great things will come from this adversity. More than ever before the services that the college pro-

vides are needed by the citizens of south Mississippi.

PRCC will help our region of the state to rebuild, to become more productive and beautiful than ever. While we wish that this monster storm had not unleashed its fury on us, we will emerge a stronger and more focused institution...

Please know that PRCC will continue to strive to be an institution where the spirit of family is demonstrated each and every day. We will do our best to support our students, our alums, our employees and the region of our great state that we serve.

We are, again, focused on seeing great things come from the unfortunate adversity that has fallen on us.

How typically Mississippi are President Lewis' words. The residents of the Magnolia State have never backed down from the challenges brought on by adversity. This statewide attitude is why Mississippi is a special place to live and why "The River" is a special place to be. Yes, three cheers for President Lewis and the entire Wildcat family.

Did you know: Wildcat football started way, way back in 1911. The origin of today's powerful gridiron program began in 1909 with the establishment of Pearl River County Agricultural High School. Later the school became Pearl River Junior College, Mississippi's first public two year college, when it began to offer freshmen college courses in 1921.

Making its debut in 1911, the first ever Pearl River high school football team finished with a 2-1 record under head coach Blonde Williams. The first Wildcat game ever played was against Laurel in a hard fought defensive battle that ended in an uncharacteristic 5-5 deadlock. Later in that inaugural season, halfback George Pearson scored "The River's" very first touchdown.

In 1924, Pearl River fielded its first junior college football team coached by E.W. "Goat" Hale. The Wildcats claimed their first state junior college championship in 1925.

That first agricultural high school team in 1911 was the forerunner to one of the most powerful and historic junior college teams in America, accumulating nineteen state championships and two national championships.

When you talk Wildcat football there is one name that always finds its way into the conversation--Thomas Dobie Holden.

Coach Holden was head football coach at Pearl River from 1948-1966. During his remarkable eighteen year career the Wildcats won 140 games, lost 43 and tied 7. His teams won seven state championships, the first in 1949. The 1961 team was undefeated at 10-0 and finished the season ranked No.1 in the nation. Coach Holden's teams also won four of five post-season bowl game appearances.

UNFORGETTABLE MOMENT
2003

PEARL RIVER FALLS TO HINDS
ON CONTROVERSIAL PLAY

Pearl River suffered its only loss of the 2003 season against Hinds Saturday at Dobie Holden Stadium. The defending South division champion and previously undefeated Wildcats lost 31-27 on a controversial play. The winning score came off an illegal forward lateral on a kickoff with 1:25 left in the game, but no referee was in position to make the call to nullify the play. The forward lateral was later confirmed when the Wildcats viewed the game film. The River later avenged the loss with a 21-17 victory over Hinds for the MACJC State Championship.

Coach Holden was one of the first to recognize the potential of the forward pass and he even experimented with the pro-set in the 1950s, well before it became a popular formation for college and pro teams.

Often referred to as a master motivator, Coach Holden said, "My philosophy was simple. I don't coach bums. A good football player is never a quitter. He learns to take the bitter with the sweet. Isn't that what life is all about?"

Holden's 1961 "dream team" went 10-0, amassed an impressive 446 points against the opponents 47, set a national junior college scoring record during the season and went on to win the National Junior College Football Championship. The 1961 team placed two backs and a center on the Juco All-American team.

Pearl River named its football stadium in his honor in 1966 and dedicated a bronze statue of the legendary coach in 2000. Dobie Holden, the bronze man, will be remembered forever on the Pearl River campus and he is right at home next to the football stadium that bears his name.

Over the storied history of the Wildcat football program it has produced scores of players who have received All-American honors. Former

Pearl River quarterback Jimmy Oliver will be forever endeared to Wildcat fans. Recruited out of East Marion, he guided The River to back to back MACJC state championships in 2004 and 2005, including the school's second ever NJCAA national title in 2004. Oliver was a two time first team NJCAA All-American and two time Offensive Player of the Year. He signed with Jackson State and led the Tigers to their nineteenth SWAC championship in 2007. Oliver was named "Most Valuable Offensive Player" in the SWAC title bout, passing for 249 yards, including three TDs in the game.

Another Wildcat great, Willie Heidelberg out of Purvis, played at Pearl River in 1968 and 1969. As an all-state running back, he led the Wildcats to an undefeated season and state championship in 1969. Heidelberg attended the University of Southern Mississippi where he played running back for the Golden Eagles. He is still remembered for his two touchdown performance in USM's shocking 30-14 victory in 1970 over nationally ranked Ole Miss in Oxford.

Pearl River fans also remember another Wildcat great, but not for his gridiron heroics. Instead, this favorite son of The River is noted for his ability singing, playing his guitar and writing books.... "Mr. Margaritaville"--Jimmy Buffet.

Buffet, who was born in Pascagoula but grew up in Mobile, attended Pearl River and the University of Southern Mississippi in the '60s. In his book, *A Pirate Looks at Fifty*, Buffet describes how he ended up in Poplarville in the chapter "A Hippie in Mississippi." He writes:

"I had stumbled onto the school purely by accident...on that fateful day, I took the back route from Baton Rouge to Mobile...stopped at a traffic light at U.S. Highway 11 and Highway 26 intersection...I caught the eye of some PRJC coeds...I waved and watched them cross the highway onto a sidewalk and disappeared through a canopy of small magnolia trees that hung over a narrow asphalt road leading through a red brick driveway. Above the road on a archway were, the words Pearl River Junior College."

The rest is history. Today, Buffet is an international superstar earning large sums of money doing what he enjoys doing. In a *Time* magazine article, writer Eric Pooley said, "Buffet is one of only six writers to reach the No.1 spots on both the *New York Times* fiction and non-fiction best seller lists. The others are: Ernest Hemingway, John Steinbeck, William Styron, Irving Wallace and Dr. Seuss."

PEARL RIVER'S HEAD COACH ROSTER

Goat Hale 1924-1938

Dick Baxter 1939-1942

*1943

Dick Baxter 1944

L.W. Johnson 1945

James Wade 1946-1947

Dobie Holden 1948-1966

John Russell 1967-1973

Harvey Seligman 1974

J.C. Arban 1975-1985

Mike Nelson 1986-1989

Willie Coats 1990-1994

Keith Daniels 1995-2000

Scott Maxfield 2001

Tim Hatten 2001-present

No football due to World War II

Dobie Holden

Tim Hatten

PEARL RIVER   **35**
BUTLER COUNTY (KANSAS)   **14**

Coffeyville, Kansas; 2004:

The Pearl River Wildcats claimed the 2004 NJCAA Football Championship with a convincing 35-14 victory over the defending champion Butler County (Kansas) Grizzlies in the Dalton County Defenders Bowl in Coffeyville, Kansas.

The national title bout pitted No. 1 Butler, located in El Dorado, Kansas, against No. 2 Pearl River and the Wildcats left little doubt about the superiority of the Mississippi Junior College league over the rest of the country.

The Wildcats, who repeated as the Mississippi state champions with a 24-13 win over Hinds in Poplarville, dominated the afternoon in practically every facet of the game. Both of Butler's touchdowns came off Wildcat turnovers and the victory snapped a 23 game winning streak by the Jayhawk Conference champions.

Pearl River proved to have too many weapons and too much speed for the Grizzlies to handle, even though the Wildcats spotted Butler seven points in the first quarter before rolling to a commanding 21-7 lead at the half.

Pearl River finished the game with 404 yards of total offense en route to its second national championship. The Wildcats claimed their first national title in 1961 under legendary coach Dobie Holden.

COACH DOBIE HOLDEN
LEGENDARY COACH
MENTOR &
MAKER OF MEN
WHO BECAME
"WINNERS IN LIFE"

PEARL RIVER'S RECRUITING DISTRICT

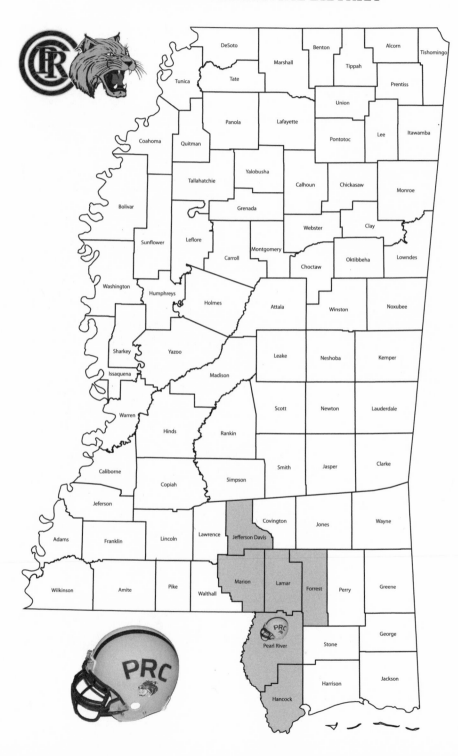

PEARL RIVER'S DISTRICT HIGH SCHOOLS

Poplarville

Pearl River Central

Picayune

Hancock County

Bay High

St. Stanislaus Prep College

Hattiesburg

Forrest County Agricultural

North Forrest

Presbyterian Christian

Purvis

Lumberton

Sumrall

Oak Grove

Lamar Christian

Columbia

East Marion

West Marion

Prentiss

Bassfield

Prentiss Christian

Columbia Academy

Petal

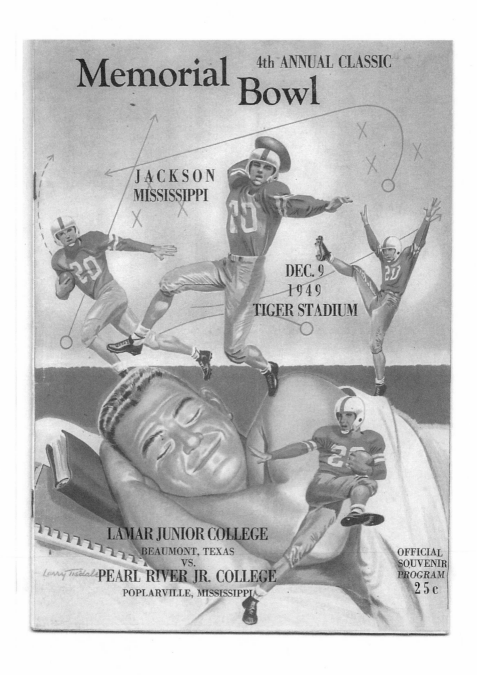

The Wolves of Co-Lin.

Mississippi Delta pursues Coahoma running back.

Southwest's mascot "Peaches" enjoying a snack.

East Central's Warrior - "Fear the Spear."

Coach Glenn Davis of Co-Lin.

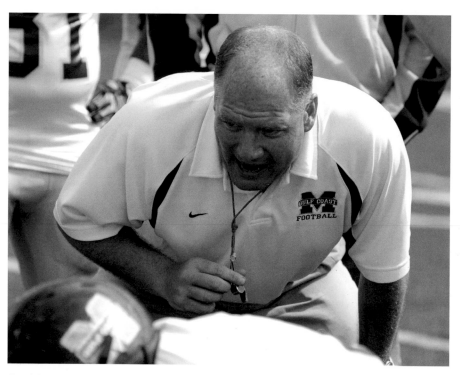

Coach Steve Campbell of Gulf Coast.

"Bozo the Great" and Hinds cheerleaders. (Circa 1956.)

The Maroon Typhoon shows its JCJC pride.

1941 Co-Lin football team.

1961 Pearl River Championship team.

1981 Holmes State Championship team.

Pregame at Southwest.

The 1966 Co-Lin Band and Colettes.

East Central fans show their spirit.

Coach A.J. Kilpatrick patrolling the EC sideline.

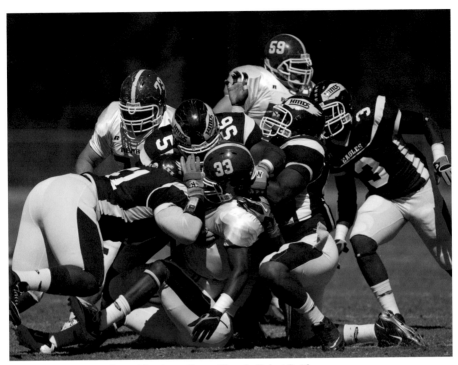

A collision of Hinds Eagles and Southwest Bears. Photo by Robert Smith

The Mississippi Gulf Coast Bulldogs take the field.

East Central player making a big play.

Itawamba Indians vs. Hinds Eagles.

Jones cheerleaders fire up the home stands.

Northeast running back looks for daylight.

Northwest Rangers celebrate an upset victory.

Pearl River's Wildcat mascot cheers on his team.

EMCC wins their first state championship in 2009.

An emotional Coach Ricky Smither and his Northeast players.

2004 Pearl River Championship team. Photo by Mitch Deaver/PRCC

Itawamba's All-American Band cheers for their team.

Jones running back Demorio Leverett.

Itawamba cheerleaders.

Hinds running back goes airborne. Photo by Robert Smith

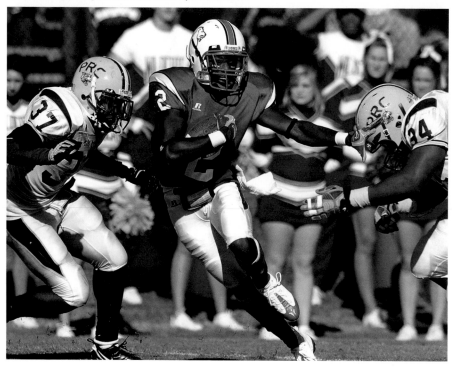

EMCC's Mike Outlaw.

Mississippi Gulf Coast's Bulldog mascot.

Northeast's Showband from Tigerland.

Itawamba's head coach Jon Williams and mascot.

East Mississippi's Randall Mackey.

Northwest's wide receiver, Myles White, breaks away from defenders.

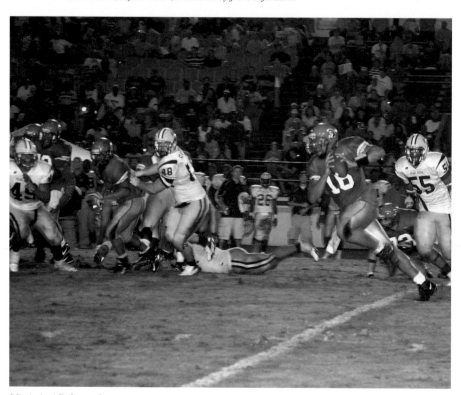

Mississippi Delta on the move.

Northeast's coach and players make their entrance.

Co-Lin, winners of the 2006 Sea Island Golden Isle Bowl.

Quarterback Emil Jones of Pearl River. Photo by Mitch Deaver

Hinds player tries to evade Jones defender. Photo by Robert Smith

Northwest head coach Ricky Woods.

East Mississippi Lions take the field in Scooba.

Southwest cheerleaders and mascot.

Northwest Rangers swarm the ball carrier.

Rabid Jones fans.

Northwest's All-American quarterback Casey Weston.

East Central Warrior mascot with his game face on.

Gulf Coast's NJCAA All-American Sean Brauchle.

East Mississippi's Sullivan-Windham Stadium.

Jones Bobcat mascot.

Hinds player makes a big gain. Photo by Robert Smith

ITAWAMBA COMMUNITY COLLEGE

Fulton, Mississippi • Founded 1948 • Enrollment 8,600

Red, White & Blue • Indians

A.C. "Butch" Lambert Stadium • Capacity 4,500

Marching Band: The All-American Band

///

PLAYING BEHIND THE BRICK WALL

The dimensions of a regulation football field for collegiate competition in the United States are standardized for all NCAA and NAIA participants. The primary playing area consists of 100 yards in length and 53 yards in width. At each end of the regulation playing field is an end zone. These end zones are both 10 yards by 53 yards in dimension. The playing field is rectangular in shape as are the end zone additions. A nice neat shape with recognizable, distinctive boundaries that everyone is accustomed to playing on.

While the majority of most football games are played on the 100 x 53 yard dimensions of the playing field, some of the most exciting action during a game can occur on the goal line, or in the end zone itself. In that constricted area the entire course of events on the larger playing field can be nullified for better or worse. Needless to say, the size and shape of a football field, whether grass or artificial turf, is important in determining a fair outcome of the contest played on it.

Remember the scene in the blockbuster movie *Hoosiers* when the coach of the small Hickory High School basketball team, portrayed by Gene Hackman, and his boys arrived in Indianapolis for the state championship

game against the heavily favored inner-city team? Hackman, noticing that his group of kids from rural Indiana was in awe as they walked into the huge arena where the big game was going to be played later that evening, called for the team's manager to get a tape measure and a ladder. He then directed the manager to measure the height of the rim of the basket to the floor along with the dimensions of the backboard.

After confirming these critical measurements, Hackman made the point to his awe-struck players standing inside the huge arena that there is nothing unusual about the set up. The size of the backboard and the height of the rim to the floor were just as they were back in Hickory. The only difference between Hickory's gym and the Indianapolis arena was a few thousand seats. But as Hackman pointed out to his players, seats don't shoot baskets and rebound loose balls off the backboard.

INDIAN TRIVIA:

The memory of the old stadium lives on with the college's "Spread the Red" tradition. The slogan is based on when the red brick wall surrounded the old stadium and the menacing atmosphere created by the crowds toward opposing teams.

Hackman displayed sound coaching strategy in calming his team and getting them to refocus on what was really important to the outcome of the impending championship contest. However, what if the height of the rim of the basket to the floor was a mere two inches higher, or lower, and the size of the basketball court was five inches longer or shorter? How would the Hickory team have reacted? We will never know because Hackman's team was not faced with this problem so any response would be just pure speculation. However, common sense and logic leads one to believe such a change to the standard dimensions of a basketball court, or any other field for organized competition, would probably result in a "psych out" moment for the participants, at least the ones who had never confronted such changes before.

For forty years football teams visiting Itawamba Junior College had to endure a "psych out" experience of "playing behind the brick wall." From 1949 until it was replaced in 1989, Itawamba's football stadium resembled a walled in brick and concrete coffin for visiting teams. To describe the stadium in the vernacular of the Itawamba mascot, Chief Winnemaw, the battle grounds for a football game looked more like a trap for unsuspecting intruders surrounded by mountains on all sides with only one way in and one way out. The escape route, however, was always guarded by literally thousands of braves from the Chief's tribe in Fulton.

The old Indians' stadium was encased in a red brick wall and concrete stands with hard concrete seating. The stands came right down to the sidelines less than ten yards from the team's benches. The light poles were planted in front of the stands and stood directly behind a flimsy wire-mesh fence which served as a make believe barrier between the fans and the teams on the sidelines. There was nothing remotely safe or aesthetically pleasing about the entire configuration of the place, especially for the visiting teams.

While the spectators were filling up the seats before kickoff the overflow crowd would take up standing one or two deep in the small area behind the fence in front of the concrete stands. By the time the teams came on the field the overflow crowd standing behind the fence would have expanded to as many as five or six deep. The fence purporting to restrain the massive crowd from spilling onto the field had the capacity to withstand a charge of eleven billy goats.

> ## UNFORGETTABLE MOMENT
> ## NOVEMBER 1977
>
> ### INDIANS SHOCK NO. 1 JONES BOBCATS:
>
> The 6-4 Itawamba Indians traveled to Ellisville to play the No. 1 ranked junior college team in America, the Jones County Bobcats, for the state title. A victory by the undefeated Bobcats over the Indians would complete an undefeated season, add another state championship trophy to the school's trophy case, and earn Jones an invitation to the Junior Rose Bowl in Pasadena, California and a shot at the national championship. In a thrilling hard fought contest, Itawamba edged Jones 13-12 to win the state title. The key play of the game was an 80-yard touchdown run by Bobby Straughter.

Once the playing of the National Anthem and the coin toss were completed, the thousands of fans bunched by the fence circling the field would start screaming blood curdling war chants and yelling words of endearment to the opposing players who were almost within their grasp. The volume of noise often reached such a level that it was impossible to speak and be heard. However, even without the benefit of audible communication it was clear to opposing players that they were to be the objects of a massacre at the hands of the Indians.

Needless to say, the conditions created inside Indian Stadium were certainly conducive to causing opponents to become somewhat nauseated with the prospect of what was getting ready to unfold. Unfortunately, there was another thought floating through the minds of many of the opposing players in addition to trying to keep their scalps--the northwest end zone.

Instead of the regulation size end zone that every team takes for granted, the Northwest end zone of the stadium deviated from the norm. As the brick wall running down the visitors side of the field approached the goal line the wall turned at a 45 degree angle instead of continuing to run straight to the back of the end zone. Consequently, a portion of the end zone (approximately 36 square feet) was clipped off the back left corner of the northwest end zone. The result was an undefinable shape using conventional geometry concepts. As if the screaming crowd hovering right over opposing players wasn't enough the undistinguishable shape of the northwest end zone added even more to the psyche out of playing "behind the brick wall."

The old stadium was demolished in 1989 but not before delivering one last magical moment for Chief Winnemaw and Indian fans. In the final game played in the old stadium, Itawamba pulled off a stunning upset of number two ranked Northwest. The victory over the Rangers kept them from playing for a national title. Itawamba's Troy Allen kicked a field goal late in the fourth quarter to ensure the Indians would end that era of football with a thrilling and shocking victory. And in which end zone did the field goal occur? That's right...the northwest end zone. Psyche out!

The old stadium with its distorted end zone was replaced with a $1.5 million new stadium and was completed for the opening of the 1990 season. The new facility is named for the late A.C. "Butch" Lambert, who was a former head football coach at Itawamba and also an SEC football official. The new stadium is surrounded by its famous hedges similar to Sanford Stadium at the University of Georgia. This venue is one of the leagues most beautiful and electrifying arenas for college football in the nation.

An overflow crowd saw the new stadium's first game on August 30, 1990, against Copiah-Lincoln. That night the Wolves from Wesson beat the Indians 17-7, but later that season Itawamba avenged the defeat by topping the

Wolves in five overtimes, 54-47, in the state semi-finals in Wesson, en route to capturing an MACJC State Championship the following week at Hinds.

★ ★ ★ ★ ★

Mike Eaton, current Administrative Assistant to the President, was the Indians head football coach from 1976 to 1992. He is the only Itawamba coach to lead teams in both the old stadium and the new A.C. "Butch" Lambert stadium. Consequently, Eaton has a unique perspective about these two gridiron battle fields, especially the old stadium.

"Yes, that old stadium was quite an imposing place for visiting teams to come and play. I used to tell our players before home games that we definitely had the advantage because we had 'em behind the wall and there was no way for them to escape," recalls Eaton.

Eaton continues, "Before one of our big games in 1978 I promised the players that if we could get a twenty-one point lead by half-time they could climb over the wall when the team returned to the field. Well, the team went crazy and jumped out to a big lead. As I promised, instead of our normal entrance to the field,

**UNFORGETTABLE MOMENT
NOVEMBER 1990**

INDIANS WIN STATE TITLE

Coming off an incredible five overtime first round win over Co-Lin, the Indians defeated perennial powerhouse Hinds on the road to win the state title 21-7.

over the wall they came much to the players and fans delight. However, there was one player, a 5'9" 300 pound defensive tackle, who couldn't quite get over the wall. So we slipped him through the entrance after the second half started."

Eaton also recalls another amusing incident that occurred in the old stadium in 1981 that could have been disastrous. "It was the Itawamba and Northeast game, which always draws huge crowds, when our student mascot, Chief Winnemaw, decided he would enter the stadium on horseback. It seemed like a good idea at the time. Of course, there was only one way in and one way out of the old stadium and both were the same way. During pre-game the bands from both schools duke it out in a battle of the bands all the way up to kickoff. It really creates an exciting atmosphere because both the Itawamba and Northeast bands are so large and good. As the Chief rode his horse through the crowd and approached the entrance to the stadium, one of the bands cranked up playing and the fans started yelling. Well, the horse got spooked and tried to turn around and exit during the pandemonium. Amidst the chaos the Chief was clinging to the panicked horse for dear life. It was a funny sight at the time but created a potentially dangerous situation. Needless to say, that was the last time the Chief rode a horse into the one-way entrance to the old stadium," laughs Eaton.

ITAWAMBA'S HEAD COACH ROSTER

A.C. "Butch" Lambert 1949 - 1950

Percy "Slick" Williamson 1951

Lawrence Matulich 1952-1953

Ray Thornton 1954-1955

Dudley Miller 1956-1972

Ben Jones 1973-1975

Mike Eaton 1976-1992

Jay Miller 1993-2001

Jeff Terrill 2002-2009

Jon Williams 2010-present

Mike Eaton

EPIC G★MES

ITAWAMBA   **54** (5 OT)
COPIAH-LINCOLN   **47**

Wesson, MS, 1990:

The Indians started the 1990 season with a loss to Co-Lin 17-7 in the first game played in the new A.C. "Butch" Lambert stadium. Coach Mike Eaton got the team redirected and finished the season second in the North, which meant a road trip to Co-Lin in the first round of the state playoffs.

Itawamba led 27-24 but the Wolves connected on a 52 yard field goal with five seconds remaining in regulation to send the game into overtime.

Incredibly, in the fifth overtime, Itawamba scored a touchdown to go ahead 54-47. But on Co-Lin's first offensive play the Wolves moved the ball to the Indians' five yard line. The Indians' defense did not give an inch and four plays later, Itawamba had advanced to the state championship game. The historic five overtime marathon had started at 2:00 p.m. and did not end until 7:00 p.m.

ITAWAMBA'S RECRUITING DISTRICT

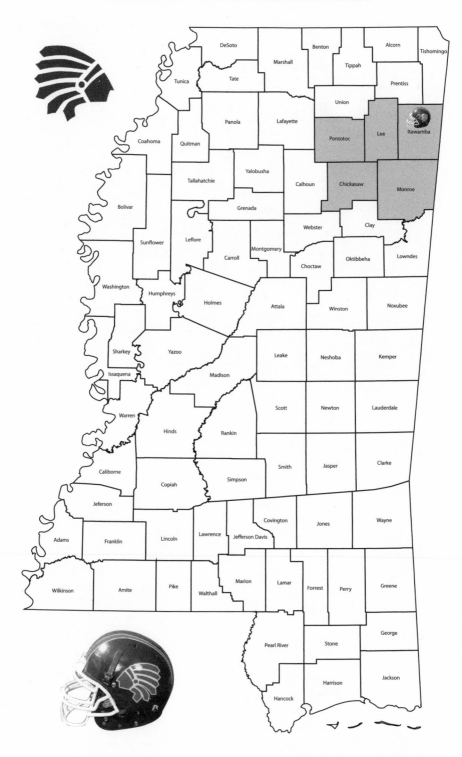

ITAWAMBA'S DISTRICT HIGH SCHOOLS

Tupelo
Nettleton
Baldwyn
Shannon
Mooreville
Saltillo
IAHS
Mantachie
Tremont
Smithville
Amory
Hatley
Aberdeen
Hamilton
Houston
Okolona
Houlka
North Pontotoc
South Pontotoc
Pontotoc
Tupelo Christian Prep

NORTHWEST MISSISSIPPI
COMMUNITY COLLEGE

Senatobia, Mississippi • Founded 1926 • Enrollment 8,800

Cardinal, Navy & Gray • Rangers

Ranger Stadium   •   Capacity 2,500

Marching Band: The Ranger Band

Chapter

10

//

WAXIE'S FIELD

Here are two trivia questions involving the Northwest Rangers and the National Football League. What is the relationship between the New York Giants, Pittsburgh Steelers, Arizona Cardinals, Washington Redskins and Northwest? Answer, nothing! No Ranger has ever been on the roster of these four NFL teams. The second trivia question of this quiz: Is there any relationship between the remaining 28 NFL teams and the Northwest Rangers? Easy answer, Oh yes! Northwest has placed one or more of its Ranger alums on the National Football League Saints, Cowboys, Ravens, Bengals, Browns, Texans, Colts, Jaguars, Titans, Bills, Dolphins, Patriots, Jets, Broncos, Chiefs, Raiders, Chargers, Rams, Bears, Lions, Packers, Vikings, Falcons, Panthers, Buccaneers, Eagles, 49ers and Seahawks.

This remarkable statistic can be partially attributed to several twists of fate. Take for example the recruiting district that was assigned to Northwest by legislative enactment when the junior college districts were first established in the '20s. The Mississippi counties in the Northwest district consist of Benton, Calhoun, Lafayette, Panola, Tunica, Marshall, DeSoto, Tallahatchie, Yalobusha, Tate, and Quitman. As luck would have it there are several high schools within the Northwest district that have what are referred to as "big time" football programs. Consider one such program, and it's as big as it gets, the national powerhouse South Panola Tigers located in Batesville only 25 miles from the Northwest campus. It certainly helps the Ranger football program that the University of South Panola, as it is appropriately referred to by folks in Mississippi, is a contender for the high school national championship almost every year. As a matter of fact, current Ranger head coach Ricky Woods led the Tigers to multiple state championships prior to taking the head coach position at Northwest.

The Northwest district is not only located in a fertile area of the state for finding football recruits, it is also squarely in an area of Mississippi that is booming economically. This economic growth is spawning an increase in population which in turn leads to the construction of more high schools. Since virtually every high school in Mississippi has a football program, Northwest becomes the beneficiary of this increased player pool.

RANGER TRIVIA:

Bobby Ray Franklin's nickname "Waxie" originated during his high school days. He and his buddy had borrowed a welding torch and mask so they could work on an old car. Franklin had applied a cream to his face to keep from blistering in the intense heat, but when he raised his mask it had melted and was dripping down his face. His buddy Hector Holcomb found the moment amusing and dubbed Franklin "Waxie" from that moment on. The nickname stuck.

Regardless of Northwest being located in the right place geographically and currently enjoying a population growth in its district, the college's football program enjoys another advantage. From its inception, the Ranger football program has always attracted outstanding coaches. However, when the topic of Northwest football is discussed one man is constantly recognized and given the most credit for the success of the Ranger program.

For 24 years, Coach Bobby Ray Franklin led the Rangers in their gridiron campaigns. Starting in 1981 until his retirement from coaching in 2005, Coach Franklin amassed a record that is nothing short of phenomenal. During his amazing coaching career at Northwest his teams won 201 games. Under Franklin, the Rangers won two national championships and were the runner-up for the national championship. Coach Franklin led Northwest to seven post season bowl games.

Current head football coach Ricky Woods readily admits Franklin is the person primarily responsible for earning the national reputation the Ranger football program enjoys today. Coach Woods says, "Bobby Ray knows everybody and the people who don't know him want to meet him. Because of his vast coaching experience and knowledge other coaches wanted to be his assistant at any position. Working for Bobby Ray was a resume builder for any coach."

To fully appreciate the long running success of the Ranger football program under Coach Franklin it helps to take a closer look at Bobby Ray Franklin, or just Bobby Ray, as most folks around Senatobia call him. But for a smaller group of close friends, Bobby Ray goes by yet another name--Waxie.

Bobby Ray Franklin was born in Clarksdale, Mississippi, October 5, 1936. He earned 12 letters in football, basketball and track at Clarksdale High from 1954-1956. During his senior year he was selected to the All-American High School team, the All-Southern team and the All-Big Eight squad. Franklin was selected to play in the Mississippi High School All-Star football game and the Wig Wam Wiesman All-American classic after his senior campaign, however, a car accident prevented him from participating.

Franklin accepted a football scholarship with the Ole Miss Rebels where he earned letters in football and track from 1956 to 1960. He was coached by the legendary Johnny Vaught. Franklin was a member of the Ole Miss squad that compiled an overall record of 35-7-1 and captured a national championship.

Franklin was an all-SEC quarterback and was named most valuable player in the 1958 Gator Bowl and the 1960 Sugar Bowl. He was the field general for the Rebel squad of 1959, which was named the Team of the Decade and won the National Championship with a record of 10-1. The one loss was the famed Halloween game against LSU and Billy Cannon.

He earned honorable mention All-American honors by UPI, played in the college All-Star game against the NFL champion Baltimore Colts and was drafted in the 11th round of the 1960 draft by the Cleveland Browns.

Franklin played for seven years with the Browns from 1960 to 1966. While at Cleveland he played with fellow Mississippi Hall of Fame members Johnny Brewer, Ralph "Catfish" Smith, Bobby Crespino, Gene Hickerson, and

Jack Gregory. His Brown teammates also included NFL legends and Hall of Fame players such as Jim Brown, Len Dawson, Frank Ryan, Paul Warfield, Dick Modzelewski, Gene Hickerson and Lou Groza. He played safety, was the holder for Groza and served as back-up punter. In his rookie season in 1960, Franklin was 2nd in the league in interceptions with eight, returning two for touchdowns. Both TDs came against the Chicago Bears and he tied an NFL record with three pickoffs in one game and returned two for touchdowns.

Franklin was a member of the 1964 Browns NFL championship team that shut out Johnny Unitas and the Baltimore Colts 27-0. He played in the NFL title game again in 1965 but the Browns were defeated by Vince Lombardi's Green Bay Packers.

Franklin entered the coaching profession in 1967 as an assistant to Bobby Dodd at Georgia Tech. The following year he returned to the NFL as a defensive backfield coach with the Dallas Cowboys under head coach Tom Landry. During Franklin's coaching tenure in Dallas, the Cowboys were in the playoffs every year. One of the players Franklin coached at Dallas was Hall of Famer, Mike Ditka. He coached in Super Bowl V and VI.

UNFORGETTABLE MOMENT
DECEMBER 1989

RANGERS DEFEAT TROJANS FOR STATE TITLE

The Northwest Rangers slipped past the Mississippi Delta Trojans 12-7 to capture the MACJC State Champiohship. The Trojans mounted a furious drive late in the fourth quarter but were repelled by a tenacious Ranger defense inside the red zone. Led by offensive guard Eddie Blake, who was called into defensive duty by Coach Franklin in the "do or die" situation, Blake sacked the Trojan quarterback three consecutive times to snuff out Delta's final drive and to preserve the Ranger's win.

After leaving the Cowboys in 1972, Franklin joined the Baltimore Colts staff under Howard Schnellenberger. For a short time, 1973-1974, he entered private business before returning as a scout for the Seattle Seahawks until he was named head coach of the Rangers in 1981.

Franklin led the Rangers for 24 seasons, compiling an amazing record of 201-56-6 including six MACJC State championships, six regional crowns, 11 North Division titles and two national championships in 1982 and 1992 and a runner up to the national title in 1991. He coached a host of All-Americans and players drafted by NFL teams. Probably the most impressive of all Franklin's records is that he had a winning record every year during his 24 year coaching career at Northwest.

Upon Franklin's arrival as head coach, the Rangers program got good quick. In his second year at the controls, Northwest completed the season 12-0-1, captured the North Division and State titles and were winners of the East Bowl with a 16-9 victory over Ferrum Community College resulting in a national championship for Northwest in 1982.

Franklin's post season play list is quite impressive: East Bowl (1982), Ranger Bowl (1986), Jayhawk Bowl (1987) Texas Shrine Bowl (1989), Mid-American Bowl (1991), Mid-American Bowl (1992), Mineral Water Bowl (1998) and the Magnolia Bowl (1999). In the previous 16 years before Franklin's arrival the Rangers had played in one post season bowl game, a 1966 appearance in the Texas Shrine Bowl.

Bobby Ray Franklin will go down in the records as one of the winningest Juco football coaches in history. He is considered the "gold standard" among junior college coaches across America.

The personal honors accumulated by Franklin as a player and

> ## UNFORGETTABLE MOMENT
> ## SEPTEMBER 2000
>
> ### NORTHWEST BURIES
> ### JONES BOBCATS
>
> The Northwest Rangers used an unstoppable aerial attack Saturday night in Laurel to bury the Jones Bobcats 72-7. Jones Coach Parker Dykes could not find the defensive combination to slow down the Ranger's quarterback, Will Hall, and his talented core of wide receivers. Asked why he didn't pull his talented quarterback when the game was out of reach, Ranger head coach Bobby Ray Franklin explained, "Both our back-up quarterbacks were hurt, Hall's all we had left."

coach are staggering. He was named as the NJCAA Coach of the Year in 1982 and 1992. Schutts Sports named him the National Junior College Coach of the Year in 2000. Franklin has been inducted into the Ole Miss Athletic Hall of Fame, the Northwest Community College Hall of Fame, the National Junior College Athletic Association Hall of Fame, Mississippi Coaches Hall of Fame, Mississippi Community College Hall of Fame and the Mississippi Sports Hall of Fame.

Two honors in particular underscore the impact of Franklin on the world of Juco football, both on a local and national level. In 1999, he was honored again by the All-American Football Foundation after receiving its Unsung Hero Award in 1997. Northwest honored Franklin by naming the field at Ranger Stadium after him. The stadium is officially known as Ranger Stadium at Bobby Franklin Field.

After so many honors, accomplishments, championships, titles and crowns its insightful to learn of one of the things that gave Franklin the most pleasure as a coach at Northwest, a simple thing that so many coaches can relate to--taking care of the field. Yes, Franklin's joy was that patch of real estate comprising what was later to be his namesake. "I've always taken care of my own yard and take pride in its appearance. I like to cut grass and work the flowerbeds. As a result of the attention to the details, my home has won several 'Yard of the Month' awards in my neighborhood. Well, I just couldn't change my habits when it came to the field at Ranger Stadium. I wanted it to look like a 'Yard of the Month' too. So I cut the grass, pushed the paint machine to make sure the lines were straight, and painted the end zones for every game I coached at Northwest. Even when I retired from coaching I still cut the grass. I guess I'm addicted to the smell of freshly cut grass and paint," says Franklin.

While the stadium is now officially known as Ranger Stadium - Bobby Franklin Field, the insiders of the Northwest program, those who know the history and all the back stories, refer to the stadium simply as "Waxie's Field."

One of Franklin's biggest admirers is current head coach Ricky Woods. Let's move the spotlight off of Bobby Ray and on to Coach Woods, and the first to do so is Franklin. While everyone acknowledges Franklin is a legend, it takes someone with experience, confidence and a high degree of self worth to follow a legend. Most coaches would not, or maybe more appropriately, could not do it. Not only has Coach Woods stepped in to take control of the high powered Ranger football program he has revved it up another notch.

Since becoming head coach in 2008, Woods' Ranger teams have posted winning records through three seasons while capturing a North Division title in 2010 with an undefeated regular season and a No. 6 NJCAA final ranking.

Ricky Woods has the same champion mentality as Franklin and harbors a deep respect for the Rangers' national reputation created by the work of his predecessor. Coach Woods does not intend to let Waxie down--and he won't!

★ ★ ★ ★ ★

During Franklin's first year (1981) as head coach of the Rangers he recalls a rather humorous incident that took place at the first home game of the season. "Someone donated a black stallion to the college for the Ranger mascot to ride, who was a student dressed in cowboy attire. The idea was for the Ranger to ride around the stadium helping fire up the home crowd," recalls Franklin.

However, there was another custom at Northwest at the time the stallion was unleashed. A cannon was fired each time the Rangers scored and its discharge made quite a loud boom that reverberated throughout the stadium.

According to Franklin, the black stallion and the Ranger rider were a big hit during pre-game and at kickoff. Then the Rangers scored and the cannon was fired. The stallion reared up, throwing the Ranger to the ground, and off it went. In full stride the "winged horse" jumped the fence in the South end zone and galloped off into the night. The beautiful, four-legged black beast was never seen again.

NORTHWEST COMMUNITY COLLEGE   **34**
NORTHEAST OKLAHOMA A&M   **0**

Tulsa, Oklahoma, 1992:

The Northwest Rangers won their second National Championship with a decisive 34-0 win over Northeastern Oklahoma A&M in the Coca-Cola Mid-American Bowl, December 5 in Tulsa, Oklahoma.

Before the game started it looked as though the Rangers (13-0) would have to battle two foes, the Golden Norsemen from Miami, Oklahoma and Jack Frost. The game was played in subfreezing temperatures with sleet and snow falling throughout the contest.

Northwest won the statistics war as well racking up 336 yards of total offense, while the Golden Norsemen put together 310.

"It was a great way to end a perfect season," said Coach Bobby Ray Franklin. "Not many teams get a second chance to win it all like we did. This is a very special team and they deserve all the attention they receive," commented Franklin.

Franklin's 1982 squad claimed the national title ten years earlier.

NORTHWEST'S HEAD COACH ROSTER

Coach Gully 1928

Coach Funchess 1929

* 1930-1938

Doug Butler 1939

Lloyd White 1949

J.R. Newton 1941-1942

Coach Stiffis 1943

Coach Searcy 1944

F.H. Roye 1945

R.D. "Rab" Rodgers 1946

Frank Davis 1947

Bernard Blackwell 1948-1949

Howard Stubbs 1950

Unknown 1951-1953

Billy Jefferson 1954

Lindy McGee 1955

Bill Oakley 1956

James Jackson 1957-1958

James Jobe 1959-1961

Jimmy Vincent 1962

Charles Peets 1963

Bob Peterson 1964-1965

Billy Joe Cox 1966-1969

Ken Bramlett 1970-1974

A.J. Kilpatrick 1975-1978

Ray Poole 1979-1980

Bobby Franklin 1981-2004

Randy Pippin 2005-2007

Ricky Woods 2008-present

No yearbooks printed due to the Great Depression, so information not available.

Bobby Ray Franklin

NORTHWEST'S RECRUITING DISTRICT

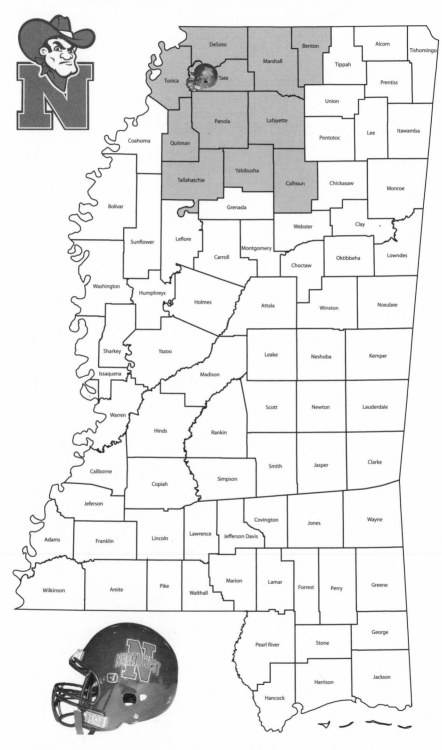

NORTHWEST'S DISTRICT HIGH SCHOOLS

Ashland
Bruce
Byhalia
Calhoun Academy
Calhoun City
Center Hill
Charleston
Coffeeville
Coldwater
Delta Academy
Desoto Central
Hernando
Hickory Flat
Holly Springs
Horn Lake
H.W. Byers
Independence
Lafayette
Lewisburg
Magnolia Heights
Marshall Academy
M.S. Palmer
North Delta Academy
North Panola
Olive Branch
Oxford
Potts Camp
Rosa Fort
Senatobia
Southhaven
Southern Baptist Educational Center
South Panola

Strayhorn
Strider Academy
Tunica Academy
Vardaman
Water Valley
West Tallahatchie

Northwest Mississippi Junior College
Official All-Sports Program • Football

RANGERS

COAHOMA COMMUNITY COLLEGE

Clarksdale, Mississippi • Founded 1949 • Enrollment 3,000

Maroon & White • Tigers

James E. Miller Stadium • Capacity 2,500

Marching Band: Tiger Marching Band

Chapter

11

//

STUDENTS.....GIVE ME A VERSE

As visitors cross the state line coming into the Magnolia State they are greeted by signs on the highways and at airports, train and bus stations that read, "Welcome to Mississippi--the Birthplace of America's Music." Arguably the epicenter for the creation of America's music is Clarksdale, a small town with a population of approximately 20,000 located in Coahoma County in the fertile Mississippi Delta.

Throughout our nation's history the Mississippi Delta has produced countless numbers of cotton crops that have supplied the fabric for the apparel worn by every American. However, it has been another by product from this region, namely its music and particularly the Blues, that has touched everyone worldwide. The international status of the little town located on the Sunflower River started during the '20s, '30s and '40s. An inordinate number of people who became icons in the music industry made Clarksdale their home. Muddy Waters, W.C. Handy, John Lee Hooker, Sam Cooke, Ike Turner, the Staple Singers family, the Five Blind Boys, Conway Twitty and playwright Tennessee Williams, resided in Clarksdale, just to name a few.

The small delta town also received attention when the first cotton crop commercially produced entirely by machinery in America was grown on land owned by the Hopson Planting Company in 1944. The international Holiday Inn franchise launched its first hotel in Clarksdale. Today, Clarksdale is home to the Delta Blues Museum, the Sunflower River Blues Festival and an unprecedented number of Mississippi Blues Trail markers commemorating individuals who have added significantly to the music culture of our nation.

Another famous landmark associated with American music culture is the Riverside Motel located in Clarksdale. Opened in 1944 by the Ratliff family, the guest books kept over the decades show that travelers from every corner of the world have been drawn to the Riverside Motel. At first glance it would appear that the Riverside Motel must have been given a five star rating by the international travel magazines. Or, perhaps, the Riverside has been designated as a discrete destination for secret meetings of delegates to the United Nations. A review of the addresses of its guests range from cities in South America, Europe, Asia, Africa and of course the USA.

UNFORGETTABLE MOMENT 2009

COAHOMA TIGERS FALL TO NATIONALLY RANKED MISSISSIPPI GULF COAST:

Facing the nationally ranked Mississippi Gulf Coast Bulldogs on their home turf in a playoff game, despite the 58-21 loss, was a positive experience for the Coahoma Tigers. In a David and Goliath matchup the Tigers never stopped playing, never gave up and kept going after points all the way to the end of the game. This was Coahoma's first time in the playoffs since joining the MACJC in 1975.

Instead of international travel ratings or affiliations with world organizations, the Riverside has developed a reputation as a mecca for musicians around the globe. Like pilgrims traveling great distances to a holy land to experience the magical influence of a special place, musicians flock to the Riverside for the spiritual experience of being where it all started--at the birthplace of American music culture, and what has arguably become the major influence of the music culture worldwide.

The list of guests at the Riverside Motel is a virtual who's who in the music business. A few of the famous visitors include Muddy Waters, Ike Turner, Honeyboy Edwards, BB King and Bonnie Rait along with some foreign guests like Bob Dylan, Eric Clapton, and John Lennon.

Today guests at the Riverside Motel occupy rooms that have essentially remained unchanged from decades gone by so that traces of past memories still linger in the air. Clothes still hang in the closets, suitcases unpacked and notebooks of musical scores sit on nightstands.

Over the years legends about the Riverside's inspirational powers have grown and musicians from around the world continue to make the pilgrimage to Clarksdale. Visitors spend a few nights to soak up the nostalgia and seek the inspiration from the many former guests who have stayed at the Riverside.

While the famous faces have come and gone there is one constant in the midst of the comings and goings of all the worldwide travelers--Rat Ratliff. Guests can pass the time sitting on the front porch at the Riverside listening to stories of the old days spun by Rat. Since his family opened the motel in 1944, Rat is certainly an authority on the history and events occurring at the Riverside. However, don't be surprised if the conversation starts to drift away from the Riverside and the rich influences of the Delta on American music culture. Eventually Riverside guests will inevitably be introduced to another dimension of Rat's life and of the fabric of the town of Clarksdale.

A walk around the campus of Coahoma Junior College located on Friars Point Road near the Mississippi River in Clarksdale will take you back in time. Much like a visitor to the Riverside Motel who is washed in the pure nostalgia of the place, so does a stroll across the 99 acre campus create the same "remember when" sensation for visitors. While there are exceptions to the '60s styled structures scattered across the campus, such as the state-of-the-art Pinnacle Coliseum, the feel of the campus is very much of the old days.

The combination of the spartan appearance of the campus with the isolation of the college in the remote region of the Mississippi Delta might lead one to believe that Coahoma Community College is unknown to most people in the U.S. and quite possibly to Mississippians as well. Surprisingly, such is not the case for two reasons. First, because of its location the college is the beneficiary of all the attention given to its famous musicians who have lived, or live, in its backyard. The college has become a repository of many aspects

of the cultural heritage of the music created by its famous sons.

The second reason that many people are aware of the small college in the Mississippi Delta is because of its Tiger football team. Oh yes, the Co-ahoma Tigers put the school on the map in the Juco football world early on in its history.

The Tiger gridiron legacy began with the college's first president, B.F. McLaurin. According to many students who attended Coahoma in those early days circa 1945-1966, McLaurin was not just the President, he was the abso-lute, supreme authority. In effect, he was a dictator, albeit a benevolent one.

Rat Ratliff, the proprietor of the Riverside Motel, remembers those early years quite clearly, "Yes, President McLaurin recruited the best athletes, students and teachers. However, if you didn't live up to your potential he

would not hesitate to run you off campus." McLaurin ran the college with an iron fist and made no exceptions when it came to his expectations of excellence.

Legend has it that McLaurin would deny students access to the dining hall if they did not make their grades. The same punishment was meted out to ath-letes who failed to attend practice or who performed poorly in games. McLaurin was also notorious for making students study all night in the library by locking them out of their dorm.

McLaurin's strictest rule, the one he insisted that every student must follow without exception, was to know the school's alma mater. He consid-ered school spirit to be the cornerstone of any great college. Consequently, McLaurin mandated that the school's alma mater be sung at every possible oc-casion and that the song be sung with great vigor by all students. His famous command was "Students give me a verse," which was followed by.....

Coahoma, Coahoma, as though the sun were rising,
Thy Precepts, thy guidance, will ever be our star;
As in the world we take our place,
Our memories of thee remain.

We'll do our best to win the bitter race and honor to retain.
Coahoma, Coahoma, thy sons are now arising
To the great call men of courage.
We shed thy light afar.

Rat recalls with great fondness his playing days at Coahoma, "Players came from Detroit, Chicago, Pittsburgh, Kansas City, St. Louis, New York, Boston and Jackson just to be a part of the Tigers' football tradition." He continues, "We rolled over every team we played. It got so bad, none of the schools in the state would play us. We had to play most of our games out of state just to get competition."

During the Tigers rein of terror, the little college in the Mississippi Delta became a household name in football circles across the country. Rat gives the credit for the success of the Tiger football program to President McLaurin. He explains, "President McLaurin raised all the money to equip the team. We travelled to away games on big Greyhound buses which were paid for from funds the President raised. He believed in sending the Tigers off in style and expected that we would play in style--which meant to win and to win big. And we did."

According to Rat, President McLaurin was real strict with all the students but particularly so with the athletes. "If you were on a sports scholarship and were not handling your business, he would come get you from the dining hall. He would say, 'You can't eat. Since I'm paying for your education, if you can't get on the books and do right, then go home. You're not going to eat my food.'"

During the time, circa 1960s, when Rat played football at Coahoma, formerly called Coahoma County Junior College and Agricultural High School, under the then existing "separate but equal" doctrine for education, there were no white students, teachers or administrators on campus. However, when the Tigers played a home game at Higgins Park not only was the stadium packed with spectators, half the crowd was white.

Unfortunately, the winning streak came to an abrupt end around 1972. Oddly, the culprit that caged the Tigers was integration. According to current head football coach and athletic director, Freeman Horton, "From 1971 to 1974, the college did not field a team. Because of integration many of the black student athletes who would have traditionally attended Coahoma opted instead to attend larger universities on athletic scholarships."

In addition, the four year hiatus from football allowed Coahoma's competition an advantage recruiting and fund raising to build new facilities. When football was reinstated, the Tigers were forced to play catchup and the result was a horrible losing steak that went on for years. Understandably, attendance at games and community support suffered greatly. Even Rat, a former player and long time supporter said, "I just couldn't bear to watch. I just couldn't make time to come watch losers play."

UNFORGETTABLE MOMENT
1994

TIGERS BREAK 82 GAME WINLESS STREAK:

The longest winless steak in junior college history finally ended October 3, 1994 when the Coahoma Tigers defeated East Central 22-18 in the historic homecoming game.

To add to the frustration of trying to rebuild the Tiger football program back to its status in the '60s, Coahoma finds itself in a recruiting district where there is only one 4A high school with the rest being 3A, 2A and 1A schools. The player pool is much smaller today compared to the recruiting territory of what amounted to the entire nation back when Rat played at the college.

Coach Horton says, "We are coming back because the kids from Clarksdale and the Delta community are used to working hard. They are not afraid to work and they will play every second on the clock. Our most important resource is the community. Now that we are starting to win again, the fans are returning. For a long time everyone thought the Tigers were dead. No more. They are alive and well."

The Tiger's spirit for a return to greatness has been greatly aided by Coahoma's current president, Dr. Vivian Presley, who has raised the funds necessary to upgrade the athletic facilities. Coach Horton says, "We don't want for anything athletic wise. We are one of the fastest growing community colleges in Mississippi." Rat agrees, "It is turning around and I support the new Tigers."

Tangible evidence that a Tiger football revival is taking place can be seen in the attendance at the 2010 homecoming festivities. Multitudes of Coahoma alumni covered the campus and attended the big game. Tailgating, plumes of smoke from grills, tents, class reunions and lots of fun...says Rat, "These people were hurting for a winner. Yes sir, the Tigers are back--watch out!"

Considering the remote location of Coahoma and its size, today only about 2,500 students, which is one of the smallest community colleges in Mississippi, the production of NFL talent coming out of the small college since the segregated glory days of the Rat Ratliff and B.F. McLaurin era is impressive. Consider the following NFL roster from Coahoma:

Clarence Harmon-Washington Redskins
Randy Baldwin-Cleveland Browns
Greg Robinson-St. Louis Rams
Walter Jones-Seattle Seahawks
Terry Day-New York Jets
Paul Miranda-Seattle Seahawks
Duane Starks-Baltimore Ravens
Germany Thompson-Baltimore Ravens
Alvia McKinley-St. Louis Rams
James Atkins-Tennessee Titans
Corey Moore-Buffalo Bills
Javor Mills-Jacksonville Jaguars
Joe Sykes-Washington Redskins
Chris White-GreenBay Packers
Jacob Ford-Tennessee Titans
Larry Hart-Jacksonville Jaguars

Judging from the above roster of NFL players along with a host of famous musicians like Muddy Waters, John Lee Hooker, Sam Cooke, Ike Turner and on and on and on...it is little wonder why the alumni from the little college in the isolation of the Mississippi Delta are proud to sing their alma mater.

Coahoma, Coahoma, our beacon of tomorrow
We will always shout thy glory
Our Alma Mater dear...

COAHOMA'S HEAD COACH ROSTER

*

John Griffith 1957

Samuel Crump 1958-1960

Oree Banks 1961-1964

George Green 1965-1969

Arthur Fielder 1970

**1971-74

George Green 1975-1981

Harold Coley 1982-1983

Amzi Burt 1984

Clarence Pearson 1985-1988

Bob Holloway 1989-1992

Melvin Eubanks 1993-2000

Freeman Horton 2001-present

Freeman Horton

* Information prior to 1957 unavailable

* * Did not field a football team

EPIC G★MES

COAHOMA COMMUNITY COLLEGE   30
ITAWAMBA COMMUNITY COLLEGE   20

Clarksdale, MS, October 23, 2009:

The Coahoma Tigers earned a winning season and their first playoff trip with a 30-20 win over the Itawamba Indians.

The wild stormy weather, wind and walls of torrential rain accompanied Coahoma Community College's march into history Thursday night with a hard fought win. The muddy "slip-sliding away" victory catapulted the Tigers into a winning season and their first appearance in the football playoffs.

To reach the playoffs the Tigers won their last three games defeating Northeast 20-14 in the last week in four overtimes and Northwest 41-36 the week before.

COAHOMA'S RECRUITING DISTRICT

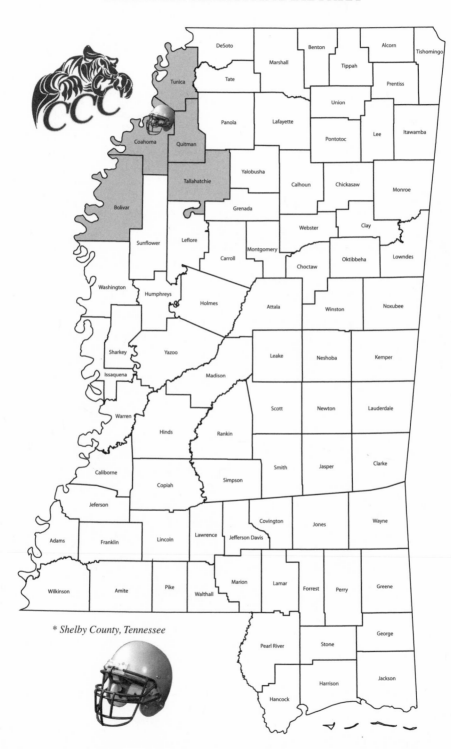

* Shelby County, Tennessee

COAHOMA'S DISTRICT HIGH SCHOOLS

Shelby Broadstreet
Clarksdale
Cleveland
Coahoma Agricultural
Coahoma County
Cleveland Eastside
John F. Kennedy
Madison Palmer
Rosa Fort
Shaw
West Bolivar
Ray Brooks
West Tallahatchie
Strider Academy
 Lee Adacemy
 Bayou Academy
Tunica Institute of Learning
 *All high schools in the city of
Memphis, TN

SOUTHWEST MISSISSIPPI
COMMUNITY COLLEGE

Summit, Mississippi • Founded 1929 • Enrollment 2,500

Cardinal Red & Royal Blue • Bears

John I. Hurst Stadium • Capacity 2,000

Marching Band: Southwest Mississippi Community

College Band

Chapter
12

//

BABY GOES TO COLLEGE

"**B**aby Goes to College".....Southwest Junior College that is. Jerry Clower, one of the most highly acclaimed country comedians and a member of the Grand Old Opry from 1973 until his death in 1998, recording artist, writer, and "raconteur," played Juco football for the Southwest Bears in 1947. "The mouth of the South" hailing from Route 4 Liberty, Mississippi describes his first experience playing football in one of his many hilarious episodes entitled "Baby Goes to College" which appears on his album, *The Best of Jerry Clower.*

Clower spins a tale about coming home after serving in the United States Navy in the Pacific during World War II. After disembarking in New Orleans he made his way back to McComb and eventually to his little hometown of East Fork, Mississippi. His mama welcomed him home and fed him then she asked, "Jerry, what is it you intend to do now that you're back?" Clower informed his mama that he was going to fulfill a life's ambition that he and his brother, Sonny, had dreamed of while growing up in their rural hometown. Apparently, the tiny school the Clower brothers attended did not have a football team so they listened to McComb High School games on the radio. Both Jerry and Sonny fantasized about what it would be like playing for the

McComb Tigers against the other big schools like Biloxi, Laurel, Meridian and Catholic High in Memphis. Jerry told his mama, "I'm gonna play football!" She responded, "Jerry, the closest thing you've ever done to playing football is kicking a milk can."

Jerry describes how he put on the tightest t-shirt he had, sucked in his 6 foot, 214 pound frame and took off for Summit to visit the football coach at the junior college there. Once Jerry arrived on campus he made his intentions known to a group of students he met and they escorted him to the football coach's office. After a brief exchange of southern salutations with the head coach Jim Shannon, Jerry got down to business and said, "I'm here to play football for Southwest Junior College." The coach responded quickly, "I'll give you a half scholarship just looking at you." Next Coach Shannon asked, "Tell me quick what position do you play?" Without hesitation Jerry answered, "I'm the man what runs with the ball." Sixteen days later Jerry Clower was not only watching his first college football game, but he was the starting left defensive tackle. While Jerry never was the man "what runs with the ball" during his football career at Southwest, he did perform well enough to earn a football scholarship to Mississippi State University.

Clower's situation was not unusual during the post-war years. As U.S. soldiers returned home after the war, many sought to take advantage of the GI Bill to obtain a college education. A number of these veterans wanted, like Jerry, to fulfill dreams that had been interrupted by their military service. Playing football also served as an economic mechanism to help pay for a college education. The junior colleges were particularly appealing to the veterans who returned home to rural areas and wanted to stay close to family and friends from whom they had been separated during the war. And, for many of these war veterans, they found the junior college leagues, especially the Mississippi Juco league, appropriately rough and tough to satisfy their desire to play football.

Southwest Junior College is located near Summit, Mississippi, a small town in Pike County. The town originated as a railroad town and was named

Summit because it was thought to be the highest point on the Illinois Central railroad between New Orleans and Jackson, Mississippi. Today, the population of Summit, not including the students at Southwest, is approximately 1500. Mayor Percy Robinson, a graduate of Southwest and long time resident, says, "We have two popular restaurants in Summit, the Star Drive-In and Doretha's. They both fill your plate." Summit is one of those throwback towns where living is quiet, easy and crime free.

Back in the late 1800s people were flocking to Summit. Fabius Godbold dug a well on property that is now Southwest Community College to supply water for the local sawmill. The water had a strange odor and taste so it was analyzed and it was found to have a high calcium content. Word spread that the water proved beneficial for stomach, liver and kidney ailments and

by 1910 a resort named Godbold Mineral Wells was established. The owners of the resort planned to make Godbold Mineral Wells the "Coney Island of the South." The 160 acre resort had a plush hotel together with a golf course, tennis courts a ballpark and a 35 acre lake surrounded by cottages. While the Godbold Mineral Wells never achieved Coney Island status it was a popular state and regional resort until the hotel burned.

In 1918, the Pike County Agricultural High School was established on the picturesque grounds of the defunct Godbold Mineral Wells. The school first offered college work in 1929 and later added second-year courses in 1932 when the school became a full fledged junior college. Eventually, the high school was discontinued and the school became known as Southwest Junior College.

Today, Southwest is still located on its original site. The campus sprawls over 60 acres, includes 28 buildings, a football stadium and numerous athletic fields. The campus is very reminiscent of the resort in the 1900s. The buildings are situated around Bear Lake with lighted walks, bridges and paths connecting the buildings. Highlighting the lofty pines and hardwoods

are blooming azaleas, wisteria and pink magnolias. Surrounding the core of the campus is a tree farm of approximately 855 acres.

★   ★   ★   ★   ★

When Pike County Agricultural High School started playing football in the early 1900s, the team's nickname was the "Pilots." There is some anecdotal evidence that indicates the nickname may have come from some affiliation, or affinity, to military aviators around this time. Many of the agricultural high schools from which the state's junior colleges originated were nicknamed the "Aggies" in the early days of the schools. However, as the schools developed their own distinct identities they selected nicknames and mascots more suitable to their situation. Eventually the Pilot label was abandoned and replaced with the nickname "Bears."

**UNFORGETTABLE MOMENT
1958**

**SOUTHWEST BEARS WIN STATE
CHAMPIONSHIP:**

The Southwest Bears wrapped up an undefeated season (9-0) and won the Mississippi Juco football championship. The Bears outscored their opponents 233-56 and allowed only one team to score more than 8 points (Northwest scored 10.)

No one is sure when the first bear mascot made its way to the Southwest campus. The earliest bear mascot identified as such was John. Legend has it that John became so mean after he was drafted into becoming the mascot for the college that the administration decided to divest the school of the beast. John was given to the Jackson Zoo where he enjoyed a more spacious setting and took on a friendlier demeanor. Of course, none of this information can be verified by any eye witnesses.

John was followed by Peaches who roamed the campus circa late '40s and '50s. Peaches, as her name would indicate, seemed to be content with her mascot duties and lived for almost 20 years. Occasionally, Peaches would escape from her quarters and go on a "joy ride" through the woods surrounding the Southwest campus. Ike Barnes, who tended to Peaches, would alert campus security about the escaped fugitive and all the women and children living on campus were promptly advised to take refuge inside until the escapee could be apprehended.

Ike used several clever ploys to coax Peaches back into her cage without the use of deadly force or tranquilizer darts. His most effective technique was strategically placing two or three gallons of ice cream on a path leading back to the bear's cage. Once Peaches caught the scent of the vanilla ice cream, which was her favorite, it didn't take long for Peaches to find her way home. Only on one occasion did this recovery strategy fail to persuade the bear to return to her habitat. Ike was initially unable to locate the required two gallons of vanilla ice cream to set his trap, and instead, had to use chocolate ice cream. The mission was a total failure until Ike realized his miscalculation and made the necessary adjustment. Once the vanilla ice cream was clearly in sight, Peaches followed the path of her favorite frozen concoction back to her cage on campus.

"Charlie" succeeded Peaches in the '60s and late '70s, also living about 20 years. After Peaches passed, several grieving Southwest alumni started inquiring about a replacement bear mascot. One alumnus located a young bear at a petting zoo in Pennsylvania and asked its owner if he would sell the bear. The owner said he would sell the cub and without hesitation a deal was struck and Charlie was en route to Southwest Junior College to assume his new duties.

During the trip to Summit the alumnus and his passenger stopped for dinner at a restaurant somewhere in Pennsylvania. The alumnus went inside the restaurant and ordered a pizza. Charlie stayed in the back seat of the car sleeping soundly. Once the alumnus finished eating his pizza he ordered a dozen more pizzas to feed Charlie on the trip to Mississippi. While he was waiting for the pizzas, the manager of the restaurant asked why he wanted so many pizzas. The alumnus answered, "Oh, they're for my bear whose traveling with me." The manager smiled and said, "Sure." Charlie's driver countered with, "Mister, I'm not kidding. There is a bear in my car." The manager could not let it go and replied, "Tell you what, if you have a bear in the back of your car, I'll give you those pizzas for free." Both men walked outside to the parked car whereupon the restaurant manager was introduced to Charlie. Both Charlie and his driver were content with the outcome of the wager.

John, Peaches and Charlie were sometimes involved as unwilling participants in incidents associated with football games against Southwest's rival up the highway in Wesson--the Co-Lin Wolves. Any zoologist will confirm that bears and wolves do not get along in the wild, nor do their domesticated mascot breed.

According to sources at Southwest all the incidents that occurred involved the Co-Lin students as the instigators of the unfortunate events. No one at Southwest, including its students and faculty, but particularly their beloved bear mascots, played any role in the criminal like activity of the Co-Lin students. The Co-Lin nickname, the Wolves, seemed to fit their conduct during the week of the big football game between the two schools, at least this is the opinion held by everyone in Summit.

One of the most despicable incidents to ever take place in this old rivalry involved Peaches. According to reports from local law enforcement, they responded to a frantic caller who had just arrived at the area below the dorms where Peaches lived and came upon wolves (i.e. Co-Lin students) attempting to spray paint Peaches in a disgusting palette of royal blue and gray. Horrified at this sight, the heroic passer-by controlled her shock long enough to alert the authorities before she passed out. Both campus police and Summit law enforcement were dispatched to the crime scene but upon their arrival the pack of wolves had fled. Immediately a team of veterinary medical techs were called in to cleanse Peaches of the ugly array of colors painted on her. After Peaches was thoroughly washed and given four gallons of vanilla ice cream she was able to fall asleep with hopes that the horrific memory of the incident would be replaced with images of a thrashing of the Co-Lin Wolves at the homecoming game the next day.

On another occasion, Co-Lin students sneaked on to the Southwest campus under the cover of darkness and removed a section of the cage housing Peaches. The next morning, which was homecoming, Peaches was missing. An alert was issued to the thousands of people who had arrived for the upcoming football game. Near panic ensued when the campus was put under an evacuation notice until Peaches could be captured. Fortunately, Ike Barnes was able to locate the big bear within an hour after the alarm sounded. As fate would have it the cafeteria had been well stocked with vanilla ice cream for the big homecoming festivities. Peaches willingly followed the ice cream laden path set out by Ike back to her cage.

Larry Holmes, the current athletic director for Southwest, has close ties to the college for a number of reasons. His dad, Horace C. Holmes, was President of Southwest from 1972 to 2005, and prior to those duties served as head basketball coach and in several administrative positions as well as instructor from 1953 to 1972. Larry attended Southwest as a student athlete and after ten years as the head baseball coach was named the Athletic Director in 2005. As Larry recalls, "I grew up on this campus. I know every tree by heart." He remembers what it was like as a kid shooting hoops in the gym, running the bases on the baseball diamond, and playing rough house on the football field. Larry says, "It was the perfect childhood neighborhood; I had the whole campus as my playground."

Having grown up on the campus, Larry has experienced the week of the Co-Lin and Southwest football game many, many times. "Its called Co-Lin watch," says Holmes. "I remember students volunteering to help guard our football field the week of the Co-Lin game. It didn't matter whether the game was going to be played in Summit or Wesson, you had to be on guard. Students from Co-Lin would pour gasoline on our field to cover up the Bear logo, or paint defamatory things in our end zone, or both if they could get away with it. The students worked in teams to protect our field. One stayed in the press box to be the lookout. Another student sat down by the electrical box where the switch to the stadium lights were located. Both students had walkie-talkies, and if trouble was spotted by the student in the press box he alerted the student at the electrical box who flipped on the stadium lights," says Holmes.

He also recalls, "Dean Reid would hide in the azalea bushes down by the bear cage just in case the Co-Lin students tried to mess with the bear. He smoked a big cigar so anyone sneaking around by the cage couldn't miss the

UNFORGETTABLE MOMENT 2007

BEAR DEFENSE GROWLS:

Southwest defeated Pearl River 24-17 with the Bears' defense responsible for all the points scored. Roteddrick Cotton returned the opening kickoff 95-yards; Myrio Cotton returned an interception 97-yards; Antoine Wilkinson returned an interception 56-yards; and another turnover led to a field goal.

glow of the lit cigar or its smell."

While Charlie was still alive someone from an animal rights group paid a visit to the president of the college to lodge a complaint. The lady represented a group who was displeased with Charlie's living conditions and demanded that his cage be enlarged and fruit trees and rope vines be planted to create a more natural habitat. The cage was eventually enlarged but before the new foliage was planted Charlie died. After Charlie's passing the administration decided it would be better to have a student mascot dressed in a bear costume instead of incurring the cost to maintain a real bear. It is doubtful John, Peaches and Charlie would have agreed with the administration's decision.

The first claim to football glory by Southwest was achieved by its predecessor school, Pike County Agricultural High School. In 1923 the "Pilots" captured the first ever Mississippi High School football championship in a game played in Jackson.

It wasn't until 35 years later, 1958, that the Southwest Junior College Bears captured their first Mississippi Association of Community and Junior Colleges football championship. The Bears made a run at the state title again in 2000 but were defeated by the Hinds Eagles and had to settle for runner-up.

Southwest has always provided its athletes with modern facilities and experienced coaches but has been handicapped by its location and the boundaries of its recruiting district. To fully understand the unique role each of the colleges play within its athletic conference, one must first analyze the district assigned to the respective schools. Several components make up the evaluation of a district based purely on football competitiveness.

First, one has to consider the geographic area each school inherits in its State legislated district boundaries. A quick reference point is size. How large is a district? How many acres, miles, and in some instances, states are in a particular district? While the size of a district is important, it is not the most important factor.

Secondly, the number of high schools in each district must be reviewed in evaluating a district. One district may have a broad land mass but the assigned territory may be sparsely populated and have few high schools; which is not good for recruiting purposes. However, there is still another factor that trumps size and the number of high schools in a district.

Thirdly, how many of the high schools in the district are "football" schools? A district may have a metropolitan area included in its district with a number of schools but they may be primarily basketball or baseball schools? Again, not good from the football recruiter's perspective.

The above factors influence the "football wealth" of a district. Of course, there are always additional forces at play like shifting demographic patterns, economic ups and downs that may force some borderline athletes to play at the junior college level in order to get an education. Nonetheless, the size of the district, the number of high schools within it, and whether the high schools in a district are football savvy schools cover the major criteria for gauging the district for football value.

Coach Charles Anthony, the current head football coach at Southwest, hails from the neighboring state of Alabama. After coaching football at the high school and at the small college and junior college level in the south, including stints at two Mississippi Juco's, he has, as they say in coaching parlance, "been around the track a few times."

He speaks about Juco football in Mississippi, "Most of the high schools and coaches in the South view Mississippi Jucos as a unique feeder system to four-year universities. When a player comes out of a junior college football program in Mississippi he is a more mature player, and most importantly, recruiters know he won't quit at the next level. Juco players are appreciative of the amenities provided to players at the university level."

How does Coach Anthony make up for the sparse football district he inherited? He says, "We look for an edge, maybe its the off season training, or the type offense we run; we find an edge. Our biggest advantage is our staff, because we will take whatever time is necessary to develop a player so he has a chance to go on to the next level." Because of the extra time and attention provided by Coach Anthony most of Southwest's football players do go on to play at the next level -- just like Jerry Clower did.

EPIC G★MES

| SOUTHWEST COMMUNITY COLLEGE | 3 |
| NORTHWEST COMMUNITY COLLEGE | 0 |

Senatobia, Mississippi, September 9, 1999:

It was a titanic defensive struggle pitting the two best defenses in the Mississippi Juco league. Northwest entered the game ranked No.1 in the nation and current Southwest head coach, Charles Anthony, was the Bears defensive coordinator when the two teams clashed. Southwest won the game on a 43-yard Mac Hart field goal with 7:48 left in the game. Northwest missed a 39-yard attempt earlier in the game. In the second half, Northwest drove to the Bears' 5-yard line but Eric Powell intercepted a pass and returned it to mid-field.

SOUTHWEST'S HEAD COACH ROSTER

John I. Hurst 1929-1933

A.H. Paddock 1934

L.J. Stovall 1935-1936

I.I. Fox 1937-1938

John I. Hurst 1939

James C. Henson 1940

*1941-1945

Jim Shannon 1946-1947

H.L. "Hook" Stone 1948-1951

Glen S. Slay 1952-1956

Eulas S. "Red" Jenkins 1957-1958

Horace Williams 1959-1965

Jerry Reid 1966-1972

Floyd Davis 1973-1982

Larry Kinslow 1983-1995

Joe Wickline 1996

Steve Campbell 1997

Kenny Edenfield 1998-2000

Dom Green 2001-1005

Charles Anthony 2006-present

Charles Anthony

No football due to World War II.

SOUTHWEST'S RECRUITING DISTRICT

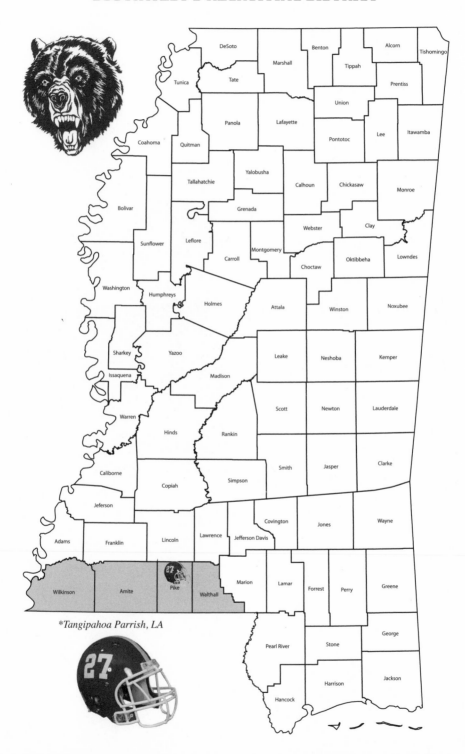

*Tangipahoa Parrish, LA

SOUTHWEST'S DISTRICT HIGH SCHOOLS

Amite County

Amite School Center

McComb

North Pike

Parklane Academy

South Pike

Dexter

Salem

Tylertown

Wilkinson County

Wilkinson County
  Christian Academy

Amite

Hammond

Independence

Kentwood

Loranger

Oak Forest Academy

Ponchatoula

St. Thomas Aquinas

Sumner

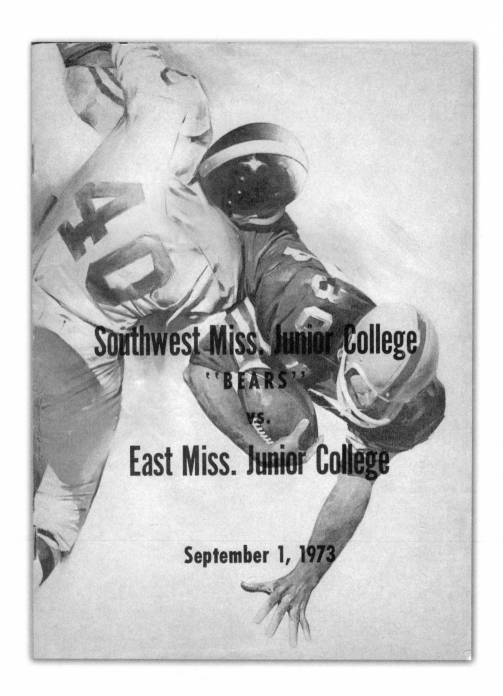

Southwest Miss. Junior College

"BEARS"

vs.

East Miss. Junior College

September 1, 1973

MISSISSIPPI DELTA COMMUNITY COLLEGE

Moorhead, Mississippi • Founded 1926 • Enrollment 3,500

Red & Black • Trojans

Jim Randall Stadium • Capacity 3,000

Marching Band: Spirit of the Delta

Chapter
13

//

VANDIVER'S DREAM

Could one football game played back in 1993 demonstrate the competitive nature of a college, a small town and an entire state? The answer is yes, and the story of how it all came about begins in 1926 with a gentleman by the name of James S. Vandiver.

Vandiver was the first president of a small college in the Mississippi Delta first known as Sunflower Junior College. The school was originally founded in connection with an agricultural high school in Moorhead, Mississippi. At the time Moorhead was a thriving railroad town near the center of the Mississippi Delta. The school's name was officially changed to Mississippi Delta Junior College in 1960. Later in the late '80s the school's name was again changed to Mississippi Delta Community College, folks refer to the school as Delta, or the modern acronym, MDCC.

President Vandiver believed in competition, especially athletic competition. He set the tone for athletics at the college from its inception when he announced, "All work and no play makes Jack a dull boy. We therefore, have one hour each day set aside for out door exercise for all students when the weather will permit. We have tennis, volleyball and basketball for the girls and football (3 teams), basketball (3 teams), tennis, track and volleyball for the boys. We work and we play."

Obviously, Vandiver was quite innovative establishing athletic teams for all the students at the college regardless of gender. No Title 9 legislation was needed at Sunflower back in the late '20s. He was outspoken about the overall importance of athletics and the involvement of both students and faculty at the college. He said, "All students and members of the faculty will buy season athletic tickets. Students must work to represent the school in literary or athletic events." In essence, Vandiver mandated that Sunflower's faculty and students become competitive, either academically or athletically. The President wanted them to go out and compete on behalf of the school and to support one another.

President Vandiver charted the course for athletics at the college and his philosophy for competitiveness guided his successors. Throughout the '30s and '40s the foundation for the men's athletic teams continued to be strengthened. The college took a major step toward achieving the competitive expectations of its first president in 1951. Long time Sports Information Director for the college, Joe Wilson, says, "When James B. Randall arrived on the scene in August, 1951, the football program was ready to take off with his guidance."

At the age of twenty-six, Randall became the youngest head football coach and athletic director in the Mississippi Juco league. Unfortunately, he inherited a team with only nineteen players leaving him with one month to recruit additional players and get ready for the first game of a grueling schedule.

Randall solicited the help of two friends. Coach Jimmy Bellipanni joined Randall to help him in the afternoons after he finished teaching at Moorhead in the mornings. A few years later Randall was able to hire J.D. Stonestreet as a backfield coach. In 1963, Coach Carl Grubb was hired after the death of Stonestreet. The trio of Randall, Bellipanni and Grubb would coach together for sixteen seasons until Randall's retirement in 1978.

Coach Randall became known throughout the state by sports writers and other Juco coaches as the "Delta Fox" because of his ability to out scheme his opponents. Under Randall and staff, the Trojans became fiercely competitive in the Mississippi Juco league winning consecutive championships in 1972 and 1973 together with North-State Division titles. The coaching trio received numerous individual and staff honors for their coaching achievements. In 1984, Coach Randall was voted into the Mississippi Association of Coaches Hall of Fame. Two years later, the Delta Fox gave the introduction for his long time friend and assistant, Bellipanni, for his induction into the same distinguished group.

During Randall's amazing 27 year head coaching career at Delta the Mississippi Juco league had become intensely competitive. The caliber of play then, as it still is today, was nothing short of awesome. Consequently, it was difficult for any one team in the league to dominate except for short stints at a time. Every game was Armageddon, so no team could overlook the next opponent on the schedule. To do so would most likely result in a defeat.

Because the Mississippi Juco league is so competitive it is extremely difficult to complete the season undefeated. When the national polls are published at the end of the regular season most Mississippi Juco teams have been tagged with one, or two, losses. Unfortunately, the pollsters tend to favor the undefeated teams and award them the top ten slots at the end of the season. However, to the well informed fans of Juco football, they well know that an undefeated Idaho team is not the same as an undefeated, or maybe two loss, Mississippi team.

In 1978, James "Wooky" Gray succeeded the Delta Fox as the head football coach at Delta. While Coach Randall remained at the college working with the Development Foundation and Alumni Association, Coach Bellipanni stayed on staff with the incoming Gray. During Coach Gray's 16 year career at the helm, his teams captured three North State titles in 1978, 1984 and 1993, an impressive 10-0 regular season and State Championship in 1993 and state runner-up titles in 1978, 1988 and 1991.

Gray and his staff, like his predecessor Randall, received numerous state, regional and national honors. But the hallmark of James "Wooky" Gray's coaching career would be the biggest game in the history of Mississippi Delta. A game President Vandiver dreamed of to establish his Trojans as a national power in athletics. The ultimate in competition--a national championship. And that is what unfolded at Pocatello, Idaho on December 4,1993 when Coach Wooky Gray and the Trojans of Delta fulfilled the 67 year old dream of the school's first president.

Delta's SID, Joe Wilson, recalls, "No one could have imagined how the season would end way back in August of 1993, when the players first reported for practice. At that time a news release by the MDCC public relations department read, 'The Trojans of Mississippi Delta Community College, backed by a strong experienced defense and an offense with only a few holes to fill, are expected to make a run at the North Division title again in 1993.'"

According to Wilson, "The Trojans were picked in preseason to finish behind perennial power Northwest--the defending National and State Champions--and ahead of Itawamba Community College. Delta had finished third in the North the year before, falling to both Northwest and Itawamba."

The 1993 season started on September 2 with a road trip to Summit, Mississippi for a date with the Southwest Bears. The Trojans cruised to a 35-7 win. All that changed seven days later when the Itawamba Indians rolled into Moorhead. The Indians came to Trojan Field slinging the football and before anyone realized, the score was 17-6 the Indians way and it was the fourth quarter. Fortunately, quarterback Stewart Patridge of Greenwood engineered two long

UNFORGETTABLE MOMENT
NOVEMBER 1993

TROJANS WIN STATE CHAMPIONSHIP, DEFEAT JONES:

The Bobcats entered the game leading the state in scoring, averaging 35.3 points a game. The Trojans countered with the No. 1 defense in the state allowing only 62 yards per game on the ground. In the end, the Deltans defense won out by only a couple of inches. Trojans 21, Bobcats 20 in overtime.

drives for touchdowns to pull the Trojans ahead of the visiting Indians 18-17 with only two minutes remaining. The Indians drove deep into the Trojans' territory before the drive was abruptly stopped when Juran Bolden intercepted an Indian pass.

The Trojans went on to defeat Coahoma 45-6, Gulf Coast 49-7, Northwest 18-0, Co-Lin 38-0, Holmes 35-0, East Mississippi 41-13 and Northeast 17-7. At one point during the season, the Trojan defense went 14 quarters without allowing an opponent to score a single point.

The Delta Trojans ended the season with a 35-28 win over a very tough Pearl River team in newly dedicated Jim Randall Stadium. They also ended the season with a perfect 10-0 record and were ranked No.1 nationally.

Next up for the Trojans, a chance to win the State Championship at home against the No.1 team out of the South Division, Jones County Junior College. The Bobcats entered the game 9-1 with its only loss coming in the first game of the season, 35-33 to Holmes.

The state championship against Jones may have been one of the best football games played by the Trojans. Delta had to overcome a deficit to tie the game at 14 and send it into overtime. The Trojans drew first blood pushing the score to 21-14. The Bobcats countered with a touchdown bringing the score to within one point awaiting the PAT. The Jones coach, Parker Dykes, decided to try and win the game by going for the 2 point conversion. The Trojan defense held and pandemonium followed.

Delta won its first State championship in 21 years (i.e. 1972), finished the year a perfect 11-0 and held on to its No. 1 ranking. Awaiting the Trojans was an invitation to play in the Junior College National Championship Game against--anybody--it didn't matter.

The National Championship Game had all the typical implications riding on the outcome of it, but for Delta there were bigger stakes. First, by winning the national championship, the dream of President Vandiver and the succession of presidents who had helped build the successful athletic program at Delta would be fulfilled some 67 years later. Secondly, claiming the championship for the Trojans would validate the 27 year effort of Coach Randall and his assistants, Bellipanni and Grubb, in achieving respectability for the program on the field. Thirdly, the reputation of the Mississippi Juco League had to be protected at all costs. And, finally, the town of Moorhead and the entire state of Mississippi had a stake in this game. Often maligned by the national media for being the state with the poorest, fattest, dumbest, most racially intolerant and so on... Mississippians possess a deep, heartfelt pride for their state--its culture and heritage. A main component of their culture is football--football at any level. There is one thing Mississippians are confident in, and that is football played in the Magnolia State is the best in the nation.

Consequently, the Trojan team traveling to Pocatello, Idaho to play in the National Championship Game did so with a truck load of passion, motivation and confidence. The game was to be played at Idaho State University's 12,000 seat Holt Arena, one of the first covered college football stadiums in

the nation.

Idaho State University at Pocatello is surrounded on three sides by mountains. The first snows of winter had dusted the mountains and the town when the Trojans plane landed. The team was happy to see at least two friendly faces waiting for them when they arrived, former Trojans' quarterback Virgil Gardner and receiver Sam Carter, both of whom were playing football at Idaho State University.

According to Delta's SID, Joe Wilson, "The game was hailed by the local press as pure 'David vs Goliath.' Here was little ole MDCC with its 1200 students and 54 football players (all but ten from the Mississippi Delta) going up against Nassau Community College of Long Island, New York, one of the biggest community colleges in the nation with its 22,000 students and 94 football players. These players were the cream of the crop, selected from all along the Eastern seaboard."

But, as Coach Gray said at a press conference the day before the game, "You can only put 11 players on the field at one time, and I'd a lot rather have my 11 than theirs."

Joe Wilson offers an account of the game on that Saturday in Pocatello:

The Nassau Lions like the Trojans had dominated most of the teams they had played during the season. They had scored 318 points while allowing only 70. But, MDCC had the advantage. The Trojans mettle had been forged and tested in the heat of battle against all the best teams in the toughest Juco conference anywhere.

The game featured two very different offenses. Nassau with its smashmouth running game was up against the run and shoot mixture of passing and running of the Deltans. The Lions of Nassau took control of the game early and marched 51 yards to the Trojans' 20 before the Deltans defense stiffened allowing only a field goal. Delta responded in kind marching 75 yards in eight plays before having to rely on Channing Upchurch to tie the game with a 15-yard field goal.

It was the second quarter before Coach Gray and his staff pulled out the long range artillery and unloaded on the Lions. QB Patridge dropped back and hit a streaking Alfred Kitchens of Leland with a 55-yard TD strike. The Lions lumbered back with their running game and scored just before the half on a one yard dive that capped a 50 yard drive. The game was tied 10-10 at the half.

Delta took the lead again in the third quarter when running back Bobby Payne of Cleveland raced around the right side of the Trojans' line for seven yards and a TD. This capped a 73 yard drive that took only five plays--thanks to a 49-yard run up the middle by running back Terrance Staples of Leland.

The Trojans were headed for another TD when they fumbled on the Nassau 37. The Lions took advantage of the turnover and moved 63 yards in 14 plays for a TD. But a missed snap on the point after attempt left the Trojans on top 17-16. This was later augmented by a 23-yard field goal by Channing Upchurch with only 3:35 remaining in the game.

A premature celebration took place when the Trojans stopped the Lions on downs near the Delta 37 with only 55 seconds remaining and Delta on top 20-16. Then disaster struck.

On second down, Trojans' quarterback Stewart Patridge elected to try a quarterback sneak and run even more time off the clock instead of just kneeling

Mississippi Delta Community College

down. The play surprised the Lions and gained six yards to the Delta 45, but Patridge was stripped of the ball and Nassau was given one more chance at the championship.

The Trojans' defensive players stopped their sideline celebrations, strapped on their head gear and their determination and took to the field. Linebacker Bryan Singleton of Shaw pleaded with defensive coordinators to call an outside blitz. The coaches agreed and the next thing the Lions' quarterback knew he was looking up into the smiling face of Singleton following a 10-yard loss which left the Lions with second and 20.

On the next play, a Lions' pass fell incomplete, but Trojans Juran Bolden was called for pass interference and Nassau was given a first down on the Trojans' 39. An illegal procedure penalty on the next play moved the Lions back to the 44 and on the next play the Lions' quarterback pass overshot the intended receiver.

Then Trojan safety Juran Bolden redeemed himself for the pass inter-

ference call three plays earlier. Leaping high, Bolden made the most impor-
tant interception of his career and raced the ball back to the Lions' 36 before
being stopped. Eight seconds showed on the clock and this time there were no
mistakes.

Following the game Coach Gray said, "I'm very proud for all these kids and for the college and the Delta. I think Nassau didn't believe a little old country school could whip them, but we did."

The Trojans received many accolades in the weeks and months following their perfect season. The team paraded the National Championship trophy through downtown Moorhead and onto campus following their arrival home from Pocatello. The Trojans were treated to a fireworks display in downtown Moorhead and then walked the remaining three blocks to campus with more than 100 vehicles blaring horns and police cars with sirens going.

For their efforts, Coach James "Wooky" Gray and his staff, Jim Southward, Jeff Tatum, Terry Moore, and Domino Bellipanni, received Coach of the Year honors on both the state, regional and national levels.

One of the biggest honors for the team was a visit to the Mississippi legislature while it was in session. The Trojans received standing ovations in both the House of Representatives and the Senate before walking to the Governor's Mansion for a barbecue picnic on the grounds with Governor Kirk Fordice. Both the Mississippi Senate and House of Representatives passed resolutions honoring the Trojans' accomplishments. The Trojans' successful season was also read into the official record of the U.S. Library of Congress.

When all the festivities, celebrations and partying finally subsided, Joe Wilson posed a simple question, "What do you get when you put 54 college football players, mostly from the Mississippi Delta, up against 94 college football players from all over the East Coast? You get a National Championship for the Deltans, of course!" President Vandiver and the old cagy Delta Fox could not agree more with Joe.

"Go 'head, Mo'head!"

"If you return the bell by the end of the day the college will not press charges," stated J.T. Hall, President of Mississippi Delta.

During the '50s and especially in the late '60s a popular tradition on the campus of Mississippi Delta was the ringing of the Plantation Bell after the Trojans would score. The massive 500 pound bell was a symbolic carry over from the old plantation days. A bell was typically rung as a signal to the field workers that it was time to stop work for meals, or to end the work day. This old custom was carried over to modern days and adapted to the Trojans working on the football field. Whenever points were scored, the cheerleaders would ring and ring and ring the Plantation Bell. Of course, visiting teams and their fans did not appreciate the local tradition and would become quite annoyed with the clanging of the bell especially when their team lost to the Trojans.

There was one college in particular that took offense to the ringing of the bell, the arch rival of the Trojans, the Holmes Junior College Bulldogs down in Goodman. The students at Holmes tried on numerous occasions to steal, dismantle or deface the Delta artifact, but with little success. The attempts by the Holmes miscreants to steal the bell were not taken seriously by Delta's administration due to the massive weight of the Plantation Bell. It was almost impossible to remove it from its mounting in the Trojans' stadium.

Then in 1967 it happened. Several days before the annual slugfest between the Trojans and Bulldogs, the Plantation Bell disappeared from behind the locked gates of the Trojans' stadium. While there was no hard evidence to link any Holmes' student to the obvious criminal activity surrounding the missing bell, all suspicion was directed toward the dogs in Goodman.

President Hall, who just happened to have a good relationship with the Dean of Students at Holmes, called his friend to inquire if he knew anything about the missing bell. While his friend initially denied any knowledge, he promised to ask around to see what he might find out. Well, sure enough, after making a few inquires with persons of interest in Goodman, the Holmes' Dean was led to a local welding shop. As it turned out, the shop's owner just happened to have a son attending Holmes at the time.

Upon inquiry with the welding shop owner, the Dean was told of a rather large bell that had been delivered to the shop by his son and his friends the previous day. After the Dean informed the proprietor of the situation the custodian of the bell agreed to cooperate in assisting the Dean with getting the bell back to its rightful owner.

The shop owner informed the Dean that the gang of thieves were due to return to his shop at 9:30 the next morning. President Hall was advised of the plan and given the telephone number of the welding shop along with the name of the ring leader.

The next morning promptly at 9:30, President Hall called the welding shop in Goodman and asked to speak to the ring leader. When the Holmes student took the phone and said, "Hello," President Hall said in a calm but very authoritative voice, "We know who you are and everyone in your group that stole the Plantation Bell. The Highway Patrol has been notified and they will be sending troopers to Goodman to arrest all of you.....unless the bell is returned to Moorhead today." Then President Hall hung up the phone before the terrified Holmes student could utter a word.

By mid-afternoon of the same day, the entire gang of Holmes students accompanied by their Dean arrived in Moorhead pulling a trailer carrying the beloved Plantation Bell. On Saturday following the return of the bell, during the game with Holmes, Delta cheerleaders made a point to ring the Plantation Bell freely without limiting themselves to the honored tradition of clanging it only after Trojan scores. The ringing never sounded better to Delta fans, but to the Holmes crowd it was pure torture.

Today the old Plantation Bell has been retired and no longer provides those joyous sounds to fans after the Trojans score, however, it still holds a special place in Delta football lore--especially for that band of thieves from Holmes back in 1967.

MISSISSIPPI DELTA   20
NASSAU COMMUNITY COLLEGE   16

Pocatello, ID, December 4, 1993:

The Trojans of Mississippi Delta Community College completed the 1993 season with a perfect 12-0 record and a National Junior College Athletic Association Football Championship. En route to the win the Trojans out rushed the Lions from Nassau 221 yards to 171 yards and out passed them 170 yards to 152 yards. At the end of the game the Deltans produced 350 yards to Nassau's 269. It was Mississippi Delta's first National Championship and one of the proudest moments in the sterling coaching career of the Trojans' head coach, James "Wooky" Gray.

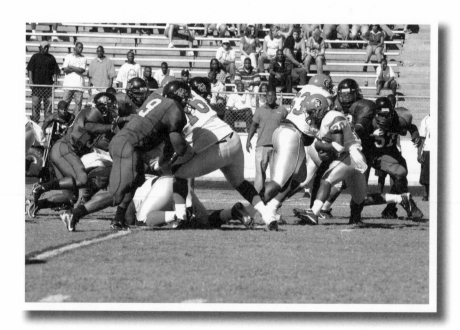

DELTA'S HEAD COACH ROSTER

*1926-1950

Jim Randall 1951-1977

Wooky Gray 1978-1993

Jim Southward 1994-2002

Jay Miller 2002-present

records not available

James "Wooky" Gray   *Jay Miller*

DELTA'S RECRUITING DISTRICT

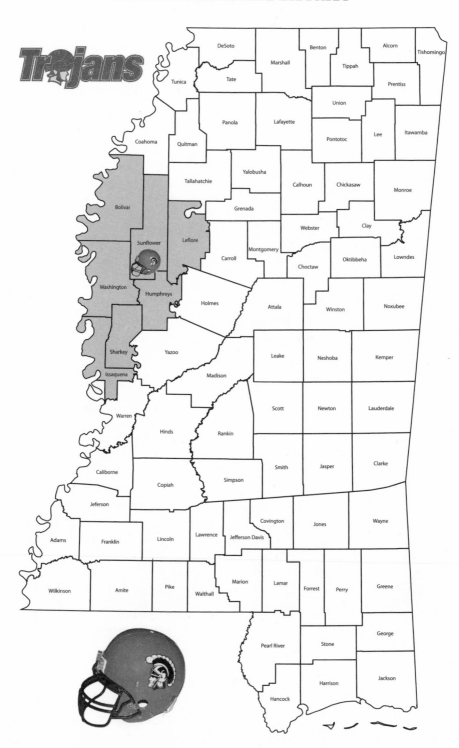

DELTA'S DISTRICT HIGH SCHOOLS

Amanda Elzy

South Delta

Bayou Academy

West Bolivar

Shelby Broad Street

Washington Academy

Cleveland

Drew

Dear Creek

Cleveland East

Gentry

Greenwood

Greenville Christian

Greenville St. Joseph

Greenville Wesson

Humphrey Academy

Humphrey County

Indianola Academy

John F. Kennedy

Leland

Leflore County

North Sunflower

O Bannon

Pillow Academy

Raybrook

Riverside

Ruleville

Sharkey Isaquena

Shaw

Simmons

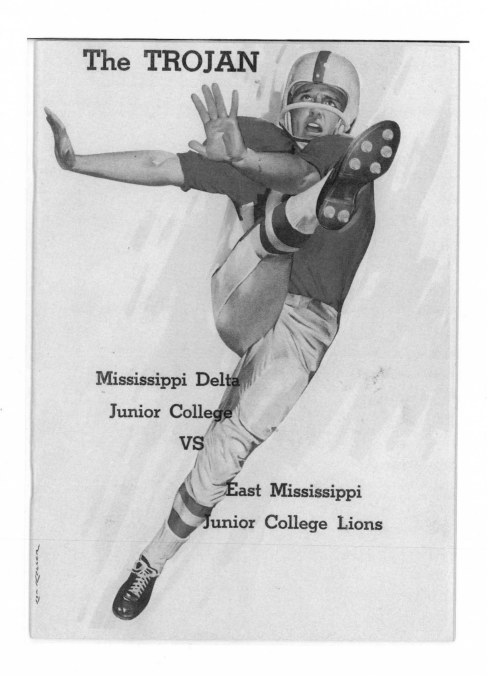

The TROJAN

Mississippi Delta
Junior College
VS
East Mississippi
Junior College Lions

NORTHEAST MISSISSIPPI
COMMUNITY COLLEGE

Booneville, Mississippi • Founded 1948 • Enrollment 3,600

Black & Gold • Tigers

Tiger Stadium • Capacity 5,500

Marching Band: The Showband from Tigerland

Chapter
14

//

WELCOME TO HILL COUNTRY

The town of Booneville is located in the northeast corner of Mississippi in the foothills leading up to the Great Smoky Mountains. Scattered throughout the counties in this part of the state are a number of Hoosier-ish little communities with the names of Walnut, Wheeler, Jumpertown, Thrasher, Myrtle, Ingomar and Blue Mountain. These mere specks on a map all have one thing in common: each have highly competitive boys and girls high school basketball teams. While Mississippi is primarily known for its powerhouse football programs, in the "hill country" basketball reigns supreme and Booneville is in the center of the hoops region. Nestled in Booneville is Northeast Mississippi Community College founded in 1948.

Ricky Ford, long time women's head basketball coach at Northeast, is a testament to the rich basketball tradition of the hill country and the influence of hoops on athletics in this region.

In 2010 he entered his 30th season as the women's coach and his 6th year as athletic director. Ford's record at Northeast stands at an amazing 588-226. He has guided the Lady Tigers to numerous north division titles and state championships. Ford began to build a powerhouse women's program in 1981, after a successful stint as the girls' and boys' coach at Booneville High

School. Coach Ford has led his teams to 15 North Division crowns, nine State Championships, three Region 23 titles, and three appearances in the national tournament, including a runner-up finish in 1986 and the 1987 National Championship. Ford has received numerous Coach of the Year honors during his distinguished career.

The Lady Tigers and Tiger basketball teams play their home games in the 3,000 seat Bonner Arnold Coliseum. Both sides of the facility are equipped with plush padded chair-back seating. The Bonner Arnold is considered one of the most menacing venues in which to compete for visiting teams. The legendary building was built in 1951 but has undergone several renovations to keep it in top condition. One of the intimidating sights for visitors to Bonner Arnold is the number of championship banners hanging overhead from the ceiling of the building.

Ricky Ford and all those banners floating overhead in historic Bonner Arnold Coliseum are all evidence of the importance of basketball to the people living in the hill country of northeast Mississippi.

Northeast is also recognized regionally for its academic success. By the early 1990s the college was offering over one hundred different programs of study to its students. One of the more unique programs, country/western music, is only one of three in the United States and the only one east of the Mississippi River. The program has received national recognition through television and magazine exposure and through student performances at national conventions. The program teaches students the basic skills necessary to launch careers in the music industry.

Northeast boasts of having one of the largest marching bands in the Mississippi Juco league. The 2009 edition of the "Showband from Tigerland" was made up of 185 instrumentalists, color guard, dancers and twirlers. In addition to the marching band, two basketball pep bands perform at all the home games.

The school has a remarkable draw of students in its five county district with over 90% of the college bound students in its district attending Northeast. In addition, after Northeast graduates transfer to four year colleges and universities, they match or surpass the academic performance of those students who start at four year schools.

How then can the Tiger football program survive in the toughest football league in America engulfed by the school's rich basketball heritage and its academic expectations? Hold your answer while you read more.

Northeast's five county district consists of Alcorn, Tippah, Tishomingo, Union and Prentiss counties. While these counties cover a relatively small geographic area this poses an additional problem for football recruiters due to their sparse population. Out of the five county area there are only 22 high schools from which to recruit. Some of these schools are so small they do not have football programs. Many of the remaining schools are in the lower size classifications, such as 1A, 2A or 3A, because of the sparse student population. Only a few of the schools in Northeast's district are large enough to be classified in the 4A ranks.

To put the problem faced by Northeast's football recruiters in perspective consider that there are more football players in Desoto County (only one county in competitor Northwest's district) than all the football players in the entire Northeast five county district. The fact is that Northeast's recruiters simply don't have the number of potential college football players available in their district to choose from as do most of the other schools in the league.

Add to the limited player pool the isolation factor and the sales pitch to potential Tiger football players gets even more difficult. Take for instance the distance from Booneville to the schools just in the North Division of the Mississippi Juco league; Booneville to: Coahoma (140 miles), East Mississippi (145 miles), Holmes (170 miles), Mississippi Delta (175 miles) and Northwest (100 miles). Only one school, Itawamba, is less than 100 miles (i.e. 50 miles). The problem is exacerbated when different South Division teams, such as Gulf Coast, rotate on the schedule creating even longer distances to travel.

The final obstacle for Northeast's recruiters to overcome is a difficult one because it is purely psychological and used to create doubt in the mind of a 17 or 18-year-old high school senior. Recruiters competing with Northeast for players might say, "Did you know that Northeast discontinued its football program in the past?" While that statement is true, the Tigers football program was discontinued for eleven years, it occurred almost half a century ago (i.e. 1957-1968). Nevertheless, once uttered and heard, the psychological seeds of doubt are planted in the fertile imagination of a teenager; "They discontinued

football before, I wonder if they might do it again."

There you have it, all the negatives Northeast's head football coach Ricky Smither and his staff face every recruiting season. So, back to the question. With all those obstacles, how does Coach Smither compete in the tough Mississippi Juco league? The answer starts many years ago with two men. Both men played football at Northeast, one went on to become a legendary high school coach and the other a legendary junior college coach, and both left indelible marks on the Tiger program. To begin to get an answer to the probing question posed, ask Coach Smither, "How do I get to Jim Drewry Drive and Bill Ward Drive?" As he gives you the directions notice the sly smile on Coach Smither's face, a sure sign that he knows something about the Tiger football program that can't be seen on the surface. To fully understand Northeast football find the streets named for the two legendary coaches, and while you are there, ask the locals about both men. After a few minutes you will start to understand that smile on Coach Smither's face.

Jim Drewry played quarterback on the Northeast Tiger football teams of 1950 and 1951. He later played at Delta State University directing the Statesmen's offense at his usual quarterback position. Following his college days, Drewry completed his military obligation in the mid-'50s. After a brief sales career with the Colgate-Palmolive Company he accepted the head football coach position at Kossuth High School in 1958.

Over fifty years later Drewry has amassed a truck load of professional and civic honors that could be attributed to a dozen men. But Drewry is quick to point out that the accolades and awards do not represent his true success. The real payoff for Drewry is that he has been successful in influencing thousands of football players over his five decade career. And, just as importantly, he has touched an even greater number of students in his classrooms.

Drewry has fulfilled his life ambition to coach and teach young people and to guide them toward becoming successful members of society. That is the legacy of Jim Drewry. Because he did it so well, everyone considers Jim Drewry to be a coach's coach.

Drewry recently received the highest honor of the American Football Coaches Association, the 2009 Power of Influence Award. The award is given to a deserving high school football coach for his positive effect on his players, school and community.

In addition to receiving the 2009 Power of Influence Award, Drewry has been inducted into the National Federation of State High School Associations Hall of Fame and is a member of the Mississippi Association of Coaches Hall of Fame. He has numerous coach of the year honors. The All-American Football Foundation presented him with the Gerald R. Ford All-American High School Coach Award in 2003. Drewry was presented a commendation resolution by the Mississippi House of Representatives in part saying, "Whereas, on October 15, 2004, Coach Drewry etched his name in Mississippi's sports history forever, when he coached his 300th career win, to become the only public school coach in Mississippi to attain the milestone....was named one of America's most winning coaches in a USA Today article in 2006....was selected Mississippi's Coach of the Quarter Century by Scholastic Coach magazine in February 2007...."

UNFORGETTABLE MOMENT
SEPTEMBER 2009

COACH SMITHER GETS BIG NORTHEAST WIN

Second year Northeast Coach Ricky Smither picked up a big win by defeating the Tiger's neighboring rivals, the Itawamba Indians. The 28-21 victory was witnessed by a packed stadium who watched the Tigers' defense recover a fumble in the end zone and return two interceptions for scores in the second half.

Since coming out of retirement and returning to Booneville in 1990 for his second stint as head coach, Drewry led the Blue Devils to three state championships (1990, 1999, and 2000), finished runner-up four other times and won three division championships. The above statistics are Drewry's post-retirement career numbers.

David R. West, Jr., a member of the Board of Aldermen of Booneville, stated the following about Coach Drewry: "It was fitting and proper to name a street after Drewry even though it was but a small thing to do in recognition of a man who has spent his life leading and encouraging young men to become real winners. He must feel great satisfaction when he looks around in our community and sees that many of his team members have continued to excel in life using those values and attitudes he fostered as 'coach'."

Drewry has always adopted the philosophy that to be a successful coach you must first be an effective teacher. Take for example Knute Rockne of Notre Dame who was an outstanding chemistry professor and Vince Lombardi who taught physics and math at St. Cecelia High School. Drewry followed the philosophy exemplified by Rockne and Lombardi and also exceled in the classroom wherever he coached. The lessons taught in his classroom

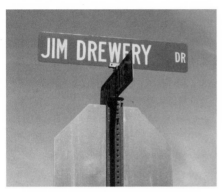

exceeded the information of the course being taught. Drewry taught life lessons to all his students. Some of his life directions that were passed on to his students are contained in quotes in the book *Gridiron Gold: Inspiring Stories of Legendary Mississippi High School Coaches, Guardians of the Greatest Football Talent in America.*

Drewry comments on the team concept:

The first play 7th graders are taught at Booneville is 48 Sweep. After the quarterback pitches the ball to the running back, his next assignment is to go block the linebacker. That's old school football.

One thing that we stress more than anything else to our football team is that there can be no I, mine or me. We're about us and ours. When I talk to the football team, I talk to them as a team and not as individuals.

We have prayer before and after every ballgame. I feel it brings the team closer together.

Drewry on "family":

Its a family tradition. The family takes such an interest in the athletes. There is closeness among the players and their parents. They all get involved. During spring practice every year, the parents are lining up on the fence, watching their kids. The entire community supports the football team.

It's the old family tradition. I've had the opportunity to coach so many players and their dads, brothers, uncles and cousins. Everybody knows everybody.

The great thing about our system is that our seventh, eighth and ninth grade teams all run our basic plays. The very first play we teach is 48 Sweep. The whole town of Booneville knows how to run 48 Sweep.

Drewry on "perspective":

We were playing Shannon on their field; and we had the ball on the three or four yard line. It was fourth down. We lined up and attempted a field goal--and missed. After the ballgame, my wife asked me, 'What were you trying to do?' I said, 'Well, I was trying to win a football game.' She said, 'That was the stupidest play I've ever seen in my life. Why didn't you just go for it and score a touchdown?' 'If I had known we were gonna miss the field goal, I would have,' I said. The very next week we played Okolona at home. We ended up in about the same situation on about the three-yard line. It was an extremely tight ballgame. I decided to go for the touchdown; but we didn't score. After the game, here she came, 'Why didn't you kick a field goal?' I said, 'If I had known we weren't going to make it, I would have.' As a head coach, you always get second guessed by everyone--even your wife. It's just part of the job.

Drewry on Mississippi Jucos:

I went through the junior college system. If it hadn't been for junior college--without that opportunity--I would not be in coaching today.

Jim Drewry, an All-American coach, living and working in an All-American town, focused on All-American values, and who helped direct over 90% of his college bound players and students on to Northeast, and all of whom arrived there with All-American attitudes. And who might be the beneficiary of Drewry's tutelage of these students and players? Maybe, in part, one Ricky Smither.

Coach Billy Ward attended Booneville High School and played center on the varsity football team from 1945 to 1948. After graduation Ward attended Northeast and played on the first Tiger gridiron team. From Northeast, Ward served in the Korean War and upon returning home he attended the University of Southern Mississippi where he joined the football team and played at his familiar center position for two years graduating in 1954.

Following his graduation Ward was considering entering the coaching profession and taking a job as an assistant football coach in Yazoo City. However, his career path changed abruptly when Ward received an offer from the school board in Booneville to return to his alma mater, not as an assistant, but as the head football coach. He accepted the job and started his long, distinguished coaching career as a head coach, and at no time ever held an assistant coach position. From 1954 until 1967, Ward coached football at Booneville, New Albany and Houston. In his thirteen years as a head high school football coach Ward never had a losing season.

In 1968, Northeast offered him the head football coach position. The Tigers football program was coming off an eleven-year hiatus. The college made the decision to discontinue football in 1957 due to a variety of reasons ranging from economics, lack of interest in the community with football and a shortage of players due to the Korean War. Nonetheless, the college wanted to reinstitute its football program and Ward certainly had the pedigree, the experience and the winning record. Ward accepted the difficult challenge of rebuilding the Tigers' program and began the next phase of his coaching career.

Ward remained as the Tigers' head football coach for 15 years until 1983, and then concentrated on his athletic director duties for another thirteen years retiring in 1996. Ward's career at Northeast spanned 28 years. He, more than anyone else, has shaped and directed the growth of not only the Northeast football program, but athletics in general at the college. Ward's fingerprints are all over Northeast's football tradition from its first team all the way down to the Tiger teams of today.

Ward's view of the world in general, and more specifically, his view of football in the hill country region of the state is priceless. Because of his life experiences as a child attending Booneville High School, playing football at Northeast and USM, and then back to Booneville High School as a head coach, Ward knows the lay of the land so to speak. While outsiders might view the football fortunes of Northeast in a negative light, not so Ward.

When interviewed for *Gridiron Gold*, Ward was asked, "Do you think the players in the small towns in this part of the state feel more pressure to win because of the legacy of having had fathers, brothers, cousins, uncles and even grandfathers playing football on the same team?" Ward responded, "Yes, I do. I played at Booneville High School. Two of my sons played there and three of my cousins. There is a tremendous unspoken pressure to win."

While Ward readily acknowledges that there are other areas of Mississippi with more football players, he likes the type of kids in Northeast's district. "Our kids for the most part come from good families who support whatever their kids do. To have a good program of any kind you must have the support of the community and of the families of the players. We get that here at Northeast," says Ward.

Ward steered the Northeast football program from its humble beginnings to a program of competitive respectability. "My main challenge was getting football on an equal level with basketball. When I arrived in 1968, the football team traveled to games in cars and dressed in the gym before home games. But, in a fairly short time, we built the program to a level of respectability. The administration never put pressure on me to win, but they demanded the program be run right and be competitive. By the time I stepped down from coaching and concentrated on my athletic director duties, the football program entered every game with a chance to win. We were, and still are, competitive," states Ward.

Ward considers Mississippi Juco football the best in the nation. "Its always been the most competitive Juco league and the roughest. No doubt it was tough in the early days and still today Mississippi Juco football is rough and tumble," says Ward.

Ward remembers a game he attended at East Mississippi when he was scouting Bull Sullivan's Lions for an upcoming game against his team. During the game, Bull had his team come out of the locker room during halftime to perform head-on tackling drills because he was so displeased with their performance in the first half. Another game involved "the worst fight I have ever seen," said Ward. "It involved everyone from the players to the coaching staffs. It literally went on for 30 minutes. At some point they started playing the Star Spangled Banner over the public address system in an attempt to get everyone to stop fighting. It didn't help. Then they started playing Dixie, and everyone started fighting harder."

One of Ward's two key principles upon which he rebuilt the Northeast football program, and upon which Coach Smither has continued, is respect for every player on the team. Ward says, "You can't demand respect, but you can gain respect by being honest with your kids. I know you can't treat every kid just alike because of their backgrounds. But you can always be honest; and you can always be fair with them. If I got on the field with a kid, and I had to get on to him at half-time or at the end of practice, I would always make a point to walk off the field with him. We always left it on the field. We didn't carry it home with us. I bet I haven't had five kids as long as I've coached who quit without coming to talk to me and telling me the reason why. If the reason was sufficient, I would go right along with them. But if it wasn't, I would try to talk them into staying."

The second principle of Northeast's legendary coach was, "I always told my players I loved them. It was easy to say because I did, each and every one of them, and so did my wife. She treated those kids like they were our own," says Ward.

Two more concepts for coaching success--respect and love--professed by another legendary football coach from the hill country. Like his friend and fellow Tiger, Jim Drewry, Ward was honored when the city of Booneville re-named Northeast Drive, which runs from Second Street to Third Street in front of the south end of Tiger Stadium, Coach Billy Ward Drive.

Two streets with names of two legendary football coaches that will be traveled by the students at Northeast and the people of Booneville for genera-

UNFORGETTABLE MOMENT
OCTOBER 2010

LIGHTING AND THUNDER STRIKE IN SCOOBA

Skies were clear and calm in Scooba Thursday, October 7, but Northeast Community college's football team let loose a rushing storm on East Mississippi and captured sole possession of second place in the North Division. The running duo of Jaquise Cook and Jamarcus Goodloe accounted for 349 yards on the ground and five scores as the Tigers knocked off the defending MACJC state champions 49-42 in an offensive storm.

tions to come. Both Coach Billy Ward Drive and Jim Drewry Drive are indeed honors for each of these men, but the real satisfaction for Drewry and Ward is that the streets provide a direction for all the students at Northeast to pursue successful lives--family, team, respect and love.

Now you understand why Coach Smither smiles when asked about the Tiger football program. All he has to do is follow Jim Drewry and Billy Ward Drives to continue the rich football legacy of Northeast, something the two famous coaches helped to create.

NORTHEAST COMMUNITY COLLEGE 28
NORTHWEST COMMUNITY COLLEGE 27

Booneville, MS 2001:

The Northeast Tigers stunned the No. 3 ranked Northwest Rangers 28-27 at Tiger Stadium in the annual slugfest. There were probably no more than 62 people in attendance who thought the Tigers had a chance to pull off an upset. Those 62 faithful fans, the Tigers' coaches and football players were proved to be right.

Freshman quarterback Ramon Burse ran for two touchdowns and threw for two more to lead the Tigers to a 28-27 victory over the nationally ranked Rangers. The win snapped Northeast's 20 game losing streak to Northwest. The Tigers last win in the series was a 26-0 shutout in 1980. The Tigers and Rangers battled to a 27-27 tie in 1993.

NORTHEAST'S HEAD COACH ROSTER

Woody Johnson 1949

Doug Hamley 1950-1951

Charles Borde 1952-1954

Horace McCool 1955-1956

* 1957-1967

William "Bill" Ward 1968-1982

David Carnell 1983-1985

Johnny Plummer 1986-1989

Hubert Tucker 1990-1994

Gunter Brewer 1995

Laurin Collins 1996-2000

Bobby Hall 2001-2002

Andy Greening 2003-2007

Ricky Smither 2008-present

Billy Ward

* No football program

NORTHEAST'S RECRUITING DISTRICT

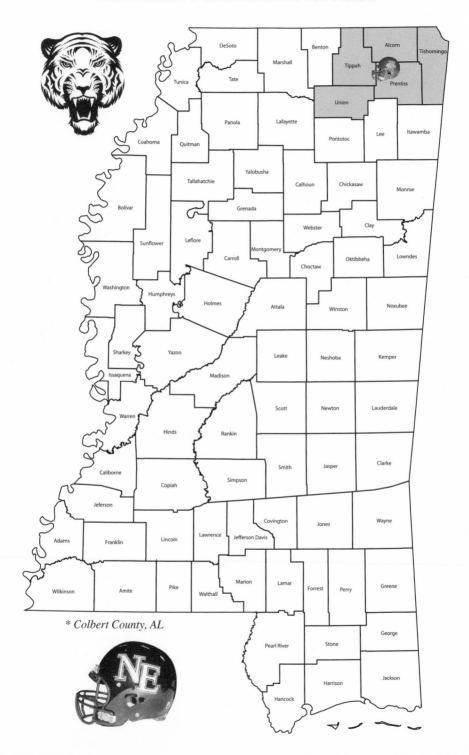

* Colbert County, AL

NORTHEAST'S DISTRICT HIGH SCHOOLS

Alcorn Central
Corinth
Biggersville
Kossuth
Booneville
Baldwyn
New Site
Jumpertown
Thrasher
Wheeler
Falkner
Blue Mountain
Ripley
Pine Grove
Walnut
Belmont
Tishomingo County
East Union
Ingomar
Myrtle
New Albany
West Union
* Colbert County, AI

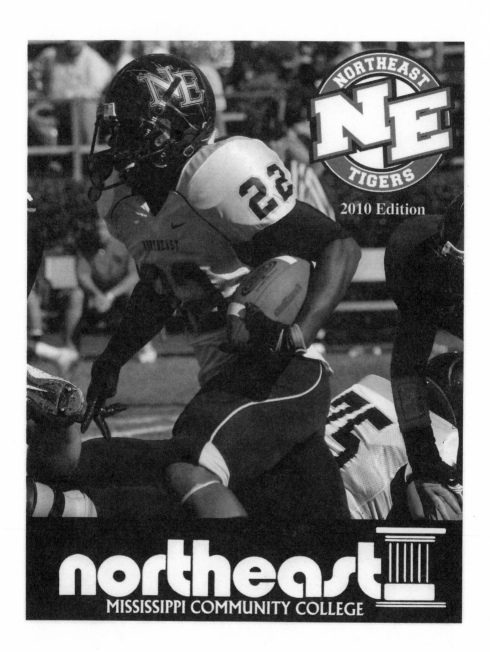

MISSISSIPPI GULF COAST COMMUNITY COLLEGE

Perkinston, Mississippi • Founded 1925 • Enrollment 10,000

Navy Blue & Gold • Bulldogs

A.L. May Memorial Stadium • Capacity 5,500

Marching Band: The Band of Gold

//

Chapter 15

A DYNASTY OF BULLDOGS

When Mississippi Gulf Coast Junior College was first established in 1925, it was known as Perkinston (Perk for short), the namesake of the town where it is located. Later the official name of the school was changed to Mississippi Gulf Coast Community College (also known as Gulf Coast).

Just 28 miles down Highway 26 from Perkinston is another small town named Poplarville which is the home of the Pearl River Junior College Wildcats. The two schools are neighbors from a geographic standpoint and both are members of the South division of the Mississippi Association of Community and Junior Colleges. However, beyond these general comparisons, any references to similarities between the two schools must be approached very delicately. Perhaps the best way to express the feelings the students at each of these fine institutions have for one another is to be candid. As many communication experts, psychologists and therapists recommend, openness, honesty and candor can often lead to better understanding between two parties whose opinions differ on certain topics. Or, as expressed in a more colloquial style, "Just put the hay down where the goats can get it." So here goes; the Wildcats of Pearl River and the Bulldogs of Gulf Coast cannot stand each other.

Their level of dislike soars to even higher altitudes when the two schools meet on the gridiron.

To try to put their mutual feelings for each other in perspective consider that the Bulldogs at Gulf Coast are often referred to by their friends at Pearl River as "coast scum." Conversely, the Wildcats at Pearl River are affectionately called "river rats" by their buddies at Gulf Coast a/k/a Perk. These two terms represent the most sanitized references one school has for the other after deleting all the colorful, descriptive, but unnecessary adjectives attached to these names.

The gridiron history of Gulf Coast and Pearl River has been tainted with controversy from the earliest beginnings of the two schools' football rivalry. It started in 1927, just twenty-four months after the two schools met on the gridiron. While neither school disputes the scores of the 1926 and 1927 games, both of which were won by Pearl River (6-0 in 1926; 13-0 in 1927), the first conflict, and a big one, centers on which school won the state championship in 1927. The 1927 football championship is of great importance to Gulf Coast because it is the first state championship claimed by the college. The basis of the Gulf Coast argument is that while Pearl River beat them 13-0 in 1927, the Bulldogs ended the year with a better record than the "river rats" from Poplarville. However, the plot thickens.

In Charles L. Sullivan's definitive work entitled *Mississippi Gulf Coast Community College: A History*, published in 2002, he addresses the controversy regarding the college's first state championship. The title to the section of his book dealing with the controversy is quite instructive, "My Vietnam--The Struggle to Find Out Who Won the 1927 Mississippi State Junior College Football Championship."

The key piece of the puzzle is the 1927 game between Gulf Coast and Hinds. If the Bulldogs beat Hinds 25-0 as the school claims, then, arguably, Gulf Coast had the best record for the '27 season and wins the championship. If, however, the Hinds victory is a misprint then Pearl River trumps the Bulldogs and the Wildcats take home the state trophy. Trying to verify what appeared on the surface to be rather easy, turned into a quagmire for Sullivan. He says, "I called Gary Higginbotham (MGCJC class of 1965), whose hobby is collecting Perk's football scores, and asked him about PRCC's claim. He said he knew about that and did not know which team won it. From 1926, when the junior college team was first fielded at Perk, Higginbotham has what is believed to be every score except for that one game--the November 19,1927 game against Hinds Junior College. Not a bad record--he lacked one game out of more than 700. I set out to find an account of that game. Over a period of five years, I estimate that I spun the microfilm of no less than 10 newspapers, no less than 50 hours and made a a trip to Hinds to check their archival holdings. I still do not have an account of that game."

After conducting additional research directed at confirming Perk's score against Hinds, Sullivan finally concluded that, "In my opinion the weight of the evidence points to Perkinston having won the 1927 football state championship."

While the controversy surrounding the 1927 championship has been laid to rest at Perkinston

UNFORGETTABLE MOMENT
DECEMBER 1984

BULLDOGS CLAIM 2ND NJCAA NATIONAL CHAMPIONSHIP:

Number 1 ranked Mississippi Gulf Coast defeated the No. 4 ranked Hartford Fighting Owls 21-7 to claim the NJCAA Championship. Coach George Sekul's Bulldogs completed a perfect 13-0 season and celebrated their second NJCAA championship in 13 years.

based on the scholarly research of Sullivan, there has been no official response to date from the Wildcat camp. Until Pearl River acknowledges Sullivan's conclusions, which will be a "terribly cold day in hell," the 1927 championship trophy will likely remain ensconced in the trophy case in Poplarville.

Fast forward to 1966, thirty-nine years after the big controversy involving the 1927 championship and note the words of David Curry, a contributor to the school newspaper, *Bulldog Barks*, under the heading "Flash--The River Rats are coming!"

"Beware, dedicated students of Gulf Coast Junior College district, a vast horde of river rats will soon descend upon your lands! Annually these loathsome creatures migrate to your area, in the manner of an ancient pestilence, to scourge and pillage your lands. For eighteen long and grueling years you have been victimized by these accursed vermin with no means of preventing their inhuman devastation. But hearken, all is not yet lost! It seems that the villains can be put to rout by large amounts of school spirit and cheering noises."

Yes, the villains were, in fact, put to rout in 1966. After seventeen consecutive losses to Pearl River (1949-1965) the Bulldogs were ready to reverse the trend of winning in their favor. It was at this point that the rivalry exploded into a more intense affair with the arrival of the new Bulldog head coach, George Sekul.

Steven George Sekul was born October 5, 1937 in Biloxi. He was an All Gulf Coast Conference Quarterback both his junior and senior year at Notre Dame High School in Biloxi. He attended Perkinston and played for head coach Harold White from 1955 to 1956. Coach Sekul attended Mississippi Southern in Hattiesburg and quarterbacked Southern's only undefeated and untied season in 1958 for the legendary coach Thad "Pie" Vann. In 1961, Sekul returned as the backfield coach at Perkinston under head coach Ed Evans.

Unfortunately, Sekul's first season back at Perk was not a good one. The Bulldogs ended the season with a dismal 2-9 record. To add insult to the abysmal record was the November 11, 1961 homecoming game against the river rats. According to Sullivan,

BULLDOG TRIVIA:

Mississippi Gulf Coast defeats Georgia Military College 41-7 to win the first ever Mississippi Bowl in Biloxi, Mississippi in 2008. The Bulldogs clinched another Mississippi Bowl victory in 2010 by defeating Grand Rapids College (Michigan) 63-52.

"This Homecoming game, touted as the gala climax of 'The Golden Years' celebration of 50 years of Perk's existence, also happened to fall on the 43rd anniversary of the end of World War I. In view of the outcome, the day was more reminiscent of the latter than the former. The Pearl River Wildcats under Coach Dobie Holden came onto the field determined to get 32 points to upset the Mississippi State Junior College record for the most points scored in a single season set by Hinds in 1951. When the smoke cleared, Holden's cats had clawed 60 points out of the Bulldogs and the Bulldogs had six. This 'cat-astrophe' set a new state record and another one as well. The Armistice Day Slaughter of 1961 still remains the most lopsided score in the Perk-Pearl River history and marked the thirteenth successive defeat of the Dawgs by the Cats."

In 1962, head coach Ed Evans resigned his coaching duties and Harold Wesson took his place. Sekul remained the backfield coach for the Bulldogs. The coaching change did not help the Perk Bulldogs against their nemesis in

Poplarville. The Wildcats defeated the Perk team in 1962, 1963, 1964, and 1965. Defeat after defeat had taken its toll on the bunch from Perkinston, but with the announcement that young George Sekul was going to take over the controls, there was new found optimism in Perkinston.

One of the first steps Coach Sekul took as the new head coach was to affiliate Gulf Coast with the National Junior College Athletic Association so that the school could compete for the NJCAA Championship Shrine Bowl Game in Savannah, Georgia.

Sekul's Perk team started the 1966 season with six consecutive wins then dropped two in a row by only one point. Carrying a 6-2 record going into the ninth game of the season, Gulf Coast was scheduled to play at Gulfport's Milner Stadium against the team from Poplarville--the same villains who put half a hundred points plus ten on the Bulldogs five years earlier during his first season as a coach at Perkinston.

The stadium was packed and the noise level almost unbearable when the Bulldogs made their appearance in Milner Stadium. The team raced on to the field led by the new bulldog mascot, Maxine. The game was over before it started. Sekul's squad played like men possessed to avenge the disastrous Armistice Day Slaughter of 1961 and the embarrassing previous 17 years of defeats. Perk rolled over Pearl River 33-0 breaking the Wildcat's death grip on the series. Perk President Hayden announced at the game over the public address system that Monday classes were dismissed declaring it a holiday appropriately named "Victory over Pearl River Day."

The following Saturday night the Bulldogs defeated Jones 21-14 at Ellisville to capture the school's first Mississippi Junior College Football Championship since 1948. The Sekul era had begun.

The 1967 season resulted in another win over Pearl River and another state championship. While Sekul's squad did not capture the title in 1968 the Bulldogs again defeated the Wildcats in a thrilling defensive struggle 7-6. Even though the 1969 and 1970 seasons produced two winning campaigns of 7-4 and 9-2-1 respectively, the Bulldogs suffered disappointing back to back shutout losses to Pearl River but redemption on a grand scale was just around the corner.

The 1971 season opened on September 4 with Itawamba and by the

time the Bulldogs reached game four on September 25 against arch rival Pearl River, both teams for the first time in history were undefeated in season play. Ironically, the big game was played at Biloxi's Municipal Stadium only blocks from Sekul's boyhood home. The Dogs and Cats fought it out for four quarters with Perk coming out on top 37-21.

After the sweet victory over their arch-rival, the Bulldogs squeaked by East Central the next week 28-27 before knocking off the remaining four regular season opponents. Then, on November 20, Perk defeated Mississippi Delta 26-14 in the State Championship Game to claim Sekul's third title and earned an invitation to play in the 15th Alee Temple Shrine Bowl for the NJCAA National Championship in Savannah, Georgia.

The opponent for the big game was the Fort Scott Greyhounds from Kansas, the previous year's national champions. Most daunting to Bulldog fans was the fact Fort Scott was not limited to a district like Perk's four county area. The Greyhounds were free to roam all over the country to find players. Their roster sported players from six states and the District of Columbia.

UNFORGETTABLE MOMENT
NOVEMBER 1986

BULLDOGS UPSET LEES-MCRAE COLLEGE IN EAST BOWL CLASSIC:

Unranked Mississippi Gulf Coast upset the undefeated 4th ranked Bobcats of Lees-McRae College 14-13 in the annual East Bowl Classic played in Conrad Stadium in Boone, North Carolina. Bulldog quarterback Danny Kelley hit wide receiver Tyrone Jones with 34 seconds left to tie the game. With the game riding on his shoulders, Adeth-sack "Sock" Chanthavane, a Croatian anti-Communist refugee whose family had been resettled in Mobile, Alabama, kicked the ball straight through the uprights to claim the Bulldog win.

Both teams came to the bowl with 10-0 records, riding impressive winning streaks (Fort Scott 27 games; Perk 17 games) and gaudy offensive and defensive statistics. The game was played at Bacon Park Stadium on a blustery, rainy Saturday night (December 3, 1971). Almost a thousand Perk fans made the trip to Savannah and were part of the 4,000 spectators that evening.

The game was a struggle the entire night with both teams delivering near knockout body blows to the other. In the final quarter, the Kansans were in range of a tying the game or pulling out a one point win. The Bulldog strategy was to burn the clock, jockey for field position and kick a field goal. Sekul's strategy worked with Perk's kicker booting a 36-yard field goal to push the Bulldog lead to the final score of 22-13.

After the hysteria on the field and once inside the locker room, Sekul told a reporter, "I've never been so happy in my life." One of the jubilant Bulldogs shouted, "We beat 'em. Four little old counties in South Mississippi beat the whole United States of America."

Sekul's dogs notched three more state titles between 1972 and 1982 and in 1984 the Bulldogs completed a perfect 13-0 season and brought home their second NJCAA championship with a convincing 21-7 victory over the Harford Fighting Owls of Maryland.

Charles Sullivan, Perk's resident historian, sums up Sekul's accomplishments at the college in a most appropriate manner. He writes, "With his retirement at the end of 1991, Sekul ended 31 seasons of service to Gulf Coast-five seasons as an assistant coach and 26 seasons as a head coach. His final tally of 204 wins, 77 losses, and 5 ties still topped the best of NJCAA football coaches' records at the close of the twentieth century."

BULLDOG TRIVIA:

The term "war daddy" refers to a football player who is not just good; he's unbelievable and extraordinarily tough. The phrase dates back to the 1950s when Harold "War Daddy" White coached the football team at Perkinston Junior College. Coach White was a legendary hard-ass.

"In the pre-Sekul era from 1926 through 1965, the football coaches of this institution produced just four state championship teams and one team that was named co-national champion. At the close of the 2000 season his successors had produced no championships of any type. Sekul won seven state championship trophies, one state co-championship trophy and two national championship trophies for the college," continues Sullivan.

"With the exception of 1943, when World War II resulted in cancellation of junior college football in Mississippi for a season, this institution fielded a football team each year from 1926 through 2000 for a total of 74 seasons. The 74 teams, which served under a total of 17 head coaches, won 417 games, lost 289 and tied 36. Sekul's 14 predecessors and two successors in 48 seasons of play established a record of 213-212-31. Sekul's record for just 26 seasons totaled 204-77-5. So, in 48 seasons, all the other coaches at Perk combined to win only nine more games than Sekul did in 26 seasons," concludes Sullivan.

Sekul's record of games won and lost, unmatched in 20th century American junior college football history, now graces the cold realm of statistics, but his legacy transcends mere figures on paper. The Sekul legacy included the lives he influenced in one degree or another--hundreds of athletes, thousands of Gulf Coast students, and tens of thousands of football fans.

The town of Perkinston has had many interesting people reside within its city limits since its founding. Few people outside of its residents are aware that this little college town has been the home of a royal family since 1924. This family of monarchs has celebrated many happy occasions while enduring their share of disappointments, even tragedy. From the horror brought on by the cold blooded murder of the royal bloodline's patriarch, the loss of one of its own to a hit and run automobile accident, to enduring impostors, and the unspeakable treachery by one of its own, this royal family has experienced it all, always sharing the good times and the bad with their subjects, the good people of Perkinston and the college located there.

The first member of the dynasty came to power in 1924. His majesty was named "Old Bob". He ascended the throne by selection of the students at Perkinston Agricultural High School who were in search of a mascot for the recently founded institution. Hence the nickname Bulldogs which became attached to the high school and its successor institution, Perkinston Junior College. Upon Old Bob's selection he was vested with powers worthy of a king. It is incontrovertible that Old Bob was considered royalty. Many Perkinstonians started referring to Old Bob and his successors as the "Kings of Perk."

Old Bob was the patriarch of the royal family. He was a large white bulldog with black eye shadow around his left eye. His appearance was regal in every aspect. Tragically, Old Bob left this world shrouded in mystery and sinister circumstances. According to a report published in the *Daily Herald*,

"An unknown gunman killed Old Bob the night of September 22, 1925." The heinous crime left the Perkinston community in shock and outrage.

Since the killer was never apprehended many intriguing theories developed as to who perpetrated this heinous act. Some people believe it was an inside job, committed by an insanely jealous person who wanted to dethrone Old Bob and replace him with a "puppet king" who would be under the killer's control. Other folks around Perkinston speculate that it was a paid hit, a professional job. This group believes that the assassin was directed by a gang of rats down the road in Poplarville. Regardless of which of the two theories seems the most plausible, the investigation into Old Bob's murder was put on hold after all the leads pursued by investigators did not produce any hard evidence. The death of Old Bob is classified as a cold case but is still open.

> **UNFORGETTABLE MOMENT**
> **DECEMBER 2007**
>
> **GULF COAST POUNDS KILGORE IN THE HEART OF TEXAS BOWL:**
>
> Mississippi Gulf Coast, ranked No.3, demolished Kilgore College (Texas) 62-28 in the 2007 CHAMPS Heart of Texas Bowl played in Copperas Cove, Texas. Gulf Coast (12-0) jumped out to a 14-0 lead on Kilgore (8-4) and rode a four touchdown performance by running back Demond Washington and 550 yards of offense to the victory and the college's first undefeated season since 1984.

It took the Perkinston community 22 years to get over the tragic loss of Old Bob. Finally, in 1947, a new mascot was offered the crown. Apparently the violence inflicted on Old Bob caused the new mascot king to cling to anonymity. Consequently the new bulldog king refused to release his name to the public during his reign. The no-name king of Perk remained in power for two years before he died of natural causes.

Duke ascended to the throne upon no-name's passing in 1949. Duke ruled for three years before his death which was also due to natural causes. Next came Buck in 1953. After another relatively short reign he too passed on due to natural causes, or so it seemed at the time. Oddly however, there are questions relating to the location of Buck's final resting place. According to Perk's historian Charles Sullivan, the only person to conduct a thorough investigation into the whereabouts of Buck's remains, he did receive a letter from a George Sherer (PJC class of 1958) purporting to have information relative to Buck's grave site. Sherer writes:

He [Buck] passed away in the fall semester of 1956. His remains are probably still where he died under Rodney Mansfield's room of the old Jackson Hall dormitory...Rodney Mansfield's room was the second from the north end of the building...on the east side...The odor was terrible. I told the college administration office about the dog dying, that he should be buried, but the college never did anything. Now, forty-one years later, I want to ask a favor from you. Would you bury Buck's remains for me? It would be deeply appreciated.

Sullivan followed the lead provided in the Sherer letter and says, "In 2000 during the renovation of Jackson Hall the workmen tearing out the floor were instructed to look for Buck's remains. Alas, no bones were found so there could be no funeral."

The site of Buck's remains still remains a mystery. The Sherer letter raises additional questions, which in turn leads to more speculation regarding what really happened to Buck. And, more importantly, why. One theory that still persists over half a century later is that there were grave robbers involved in this act of desecration. But who would do such a thing, and for what purpose? While the answers to these questions will never be known all indications point to the body snatchers residing not far from Perkinston.

King Mack followed Buck but his reign ended abruptly just 3 years later in 1961. Five years after Mack's departure, the newest member of the royal family arrived--Hail Maxine! While in power, Maxine guaranteed the continuation of her bloodline to the royal throne by birthing a litter of pups. Two of her royal offspring, Max and Jabo, were proclaimed dual heirs to the throne and remained with Maxine during her reign. Max, known as Son of Maxine, was the first of the two brothers to rise to power after Maxine's death. Shockingly, less that a year after Max took over his royal duties he was found dead one morning. Max was only 2 years old at the time of his death.

Immediately, rumors started to circulate around Perkinston accusing Jabo of orchestrating his brother's death. It was whispered amongst the folks in town that out of revenge for being passed over as the immediate heir to Maxine's throne, Jabo placed a bounty on Max's head. Of course, there were other speculations, the most noted blaming Max's death on some cult whose members were under the spell of rats. Further speculation was this secret cult lived on a commune in the Poplarville vicinity.

Nevertheless, Jabo ascended to the top dog position and assumed his role over the Perk domain. After a long, peaceful reign, Hoover replaced Jabo in 1977. King Hoover, short for J. Edgar Hoover, ruled for seven years, but very little is known about him. Hoover kept a low profile, refusing to write for *Bulldog Barks*, and only allowing a few photographs of himself to be taken. Those closest to the monarch said he lived in constant fear of being abducted and eaten alive by rats. While Hoover's nightmare never became a reality, he was the victim of a tragic hit and run accident which took his life. Witnesses to the incident say it appeared that the driver of the vehicle intentionally ran Hoover down while the monarch was crossing the street. Onlookers were unable to identify the driver of the vehicle but did note that it had a Pearl River county tag.

After the Hoover hit and run incident, a number of impostors tried to take over the duties of the royal family. For several years students disguised as bulldogs paraded around campus, especially at football games, posing as the school's mascot. This disgraceful display was endured by the true heirs to the throne and by their loyal followers. Finally, this dark period in the canine dynasty came to an end in 1991 when Mo, short for Moreover Carter Stewart, wrestled the seat of power away from the bulldog impostors.

Everything seemed to have returned to normal until an event occurred that stunned the entire Perkinston community. When it was announced that Bobby Garvin, one of the vice presidents for the college, had been named as the new president of Mississippi Delta Junior College, Mo issued a press release stating that he would abdicate the throne and accompany Garvin to Moorhead, Mississippi. The Perk loyalist were speechless. Never before in the history of the illustrious canine dynasty had one of their own betrayed the college. Mo was a damn traitor.

The Gulf Coast folks wanted an explanation for Mo's betrayal. However, neither Garvin or Mo felt the need to respond to their insulting questions. Needless to say, the rumor mill cranked up and started manufacturing possible reasons for Mo's departure. One such speculation was Garvin promised Mo that once he was president of Mississippi Delta he would banish the Trojan mascot and replace it with Mo together with providing him with a new 800 square foot doghouse. Still another outlandish speculation tied Garvin, Mo, the retiring Mississippi Delta president and another institution located not far from Perkinston, in a plot to undermine the upcoming football season by jerking Mo out from under the Bulldog faithful right before the first game. As it turned out the big loser in this soap opera was Mo. Mississippi Delta kept its Trojan mascot after Garvin assumed the presidency of the college and Mo was banished to a small 6x6 dog house in Garvin's backyard. Oh how the mighty Mo had fallen, exiled from his kingdom on the beautiful Gulf Coast to the harsh realities of the Mississippi Delta.

After the Mo incident Perk followers were in need of a strong monarch who would not only remain faithful to the cause, but one who had the courage to stand up to the river rats in Poplarville. Enter a new king, "Killer." This canine monarch served his subjects from 1995 to 1999. Upon Killer's death the throne was passed on to Mac who assumed his official duties in 2000. King Mac's blood lines were impeccable. His brother became the official "Bully" of Mississippi State University as Mac was being crowned at Perk. Mac was truly a boy king assuming his duties at the age of just 3 months old and remaining in power until February 7, 2008 when he passed away. Unfortunately, darkness again descended over the Gulf Coast domain after the passing of Mac with a resurgence of impostor kings. Since Mac's passing a human dressed in costume purporting to be a bulldog has appeared at football games parading around as if he, or she, is the chosen one. How disgraceful! Surely, Bulldog loyalists will rise up to reinstate the royal bloodline and preserve the dignity of old Bob and his successors. Long live the Kings of Perk.

EPIC G★MES

MISSISSIPPI GULF COAST   22
FORT SCOTT (KANSAS)   13

Savannah, GA, 1971:

The Gulf Coast Bulldogs and the Fort Scott Greyhounds clashed in the fifteenth Alee Temple Shrine Bowl to determine the 1971 National Junior College Championship. The Greyhounds were riding a 27 game winning streak and were the defending national champions and ranked No.1. The Bulldogs were on a 17 game winning streak and ranked No.2.

Gulf Coast raced to a 13-0 lead before the Greyhounds star running back, Tommy Raemon, got loose on a 63 yard run to put Fort Scott on the scoreboard. At halftime the score stood 13-7. In the third quarter the Bulldogs took the opening kickoff and battled down the field to score but the PAT failed making the score 19-7. Fort Scott struck back with a 12 play march resulting in a touchdown but missed the extra point because of a bad snap. The scoreboard read 19-13 and Fort Scott was within reach of tying the game and taking the lead.

In the final quarter the game turned into a defensive contest. Gulf Coast was able to grind out a 56 yard drive in eighteen plays that resulted in a 36-yard field goal by Jimmy Beck pushing the Bulldog lead to 22-13. The score held giving the Bulldogs the Bowl victory and the 1971 National Junior College Athletic Association Championship.

GULF COAST'S HEAD COACH ROSTER

W.C. "Bill" Denson 1926-1928

Lee Roy Weeks 1929-1932

C.B. "Pluck" Berry 1933-1936

Albert I. "Rex" Rexinger 1937-1941

George B. Westerfield 1942

* 1943

R.T. Walker 1944

Louis D. Megehee 1945

George B. Westerfield 1946

Marvin "Red" Campbell 1947-1948

Nolan E. Tollett 1949-1950

Robert Whitman 1951

Harold White 1952-1956

Leo P. Jones 1957-1958

Ed Evans 1959-1961

Harold Wesson 1962-1965

George Sekul 1966-1991

J.C. Arban 1992-1995

Steve Wright 1996-2001

Bill Lee 2002-2003

Steve Campbell 2004-present

George Sekul

* No footbball season

GULF COAST'S RECRUITING DISTRICT

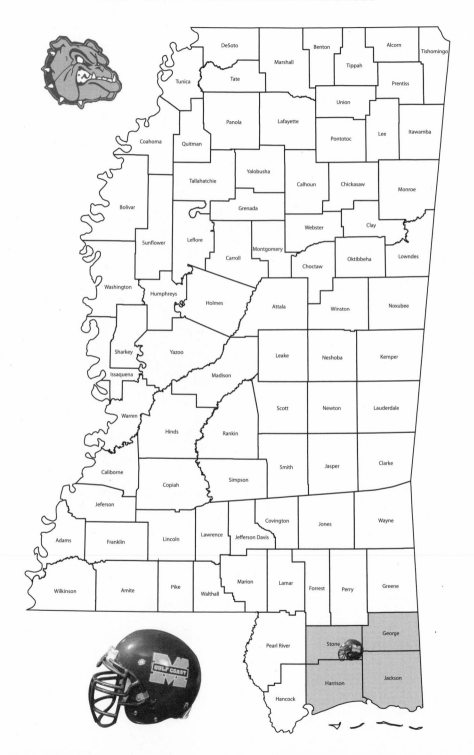

GULF COAST'S DISTRICT HIGH SCHOOLS

George County
Biloxi
D'Iberville
Gulfport
Harrison Central
Long Beach
St. Patrick
Pass Christian
Christian Collegiate
  Academy
West Harrison
Temple Christian
  Academy
East Central
Gautier
Moss Point
Mississippi Division of
  Independent Study
Ocean Springs
Pascagoula
St. Martin
Vancleave
Resurrection Catholic School

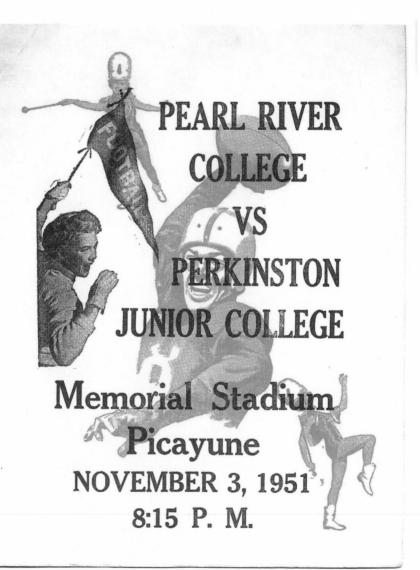

PEARL RIVER COLLEGE
VS
PERKINSTON
JUNIOR COLLEGE

Memorial Stadium
Picayune
NOVEMBER 3, 1951
8:15 P. M.

EPILOGUE

//

The Mississippi Community College System was the first system of two-year colleges in the nation. It grew out of a need to provide an education for those in the state, particularly rural Mississippi, who had no way to go off to a four-year college for "higher education." Some of the school superintendents back in the early 1920s came up with the idea to expand the agricultural high schools to provide two years of college for some of those rural areas. The agricultural high schools were in rural areas because that's mostly what the state was, rural, and that's where the problem was. Agriculture was Mississippi's biggest industry in those days.

When the legislature approved the offering of college courses at those agricultural high schools in 1922, the movement got underway, and by 1929 there were nine agricultural high schools across the state that had extended their educational offerings to include the two years beyond high school. High school football was a popular sport in those days, and the schools continued the tradition of offering that sport at the junior college level. The idea that football would become ingrained into the culture of the junior colleges was not at all foreign to the founders of the "system", but little did they know back then that football at Mississippi's two-year colleges would become the dynasty that it has become today!

Fourteen of the fifteen community colleges have a football program. It may be no coincidence that the only community college that does not have a football team is Meridian Community College. Meridian was the only one of the fifteen junior colleges that was begun through a high school initiative; all the others were started as an extension of an agricultural high school that had football as a sport. Football just never became a priority for Meridian Junior College that began operation in 1937 as the thirteenth junior college in the system. On the other hand, not one of the other fourteen colleges can boast of such success in their baseball program as Meridian. Meridian found its athletic "niche" in the system; it definitely has made baseball a major part of its culture.

Through the years the sport of football at Mississippi's two year colleges has captivated large crowds of people who follow that sport. Not only does this sport provide opportunities for athletes who are just not quite good enough to sign with a university program, it provides entertainment for those in local communities at the "next level." The ability of football players at the two-year college level has improved so profoundly over the past ninety years of Mississippi two-year college history that senior colleges and universities now pay very close attention to players at the two-year college level in that sport.

The university recruiters show up for almost every game, especially for those football games that involve teams with a winning season the previous year. As a matter of fact, there are a number of coaches at four-year colleges and universities who recommend that athletes play at the two-year college level and then transfer to the university for the last two years of eligibility. That process is commonly referred to as "farming out" high school graduates who are just not quite good enough to be awarded a football scholarship at the four-year level, but who will be good enough after the community college experience to see a lot of playing time when they transfer to the university. They know that Mississippi's two-year college football program will take good care of them and provide good playing experience before they transfer to the university. The quality of football at the two-year level in Mississippi has definitely been demonstrated by the success of those who go on to play at the university level and then at the professional level.

Mississippi community college football provides opportunities for other activities which are important to the college atmosphere as well. Almost all of Mississippi's community colleges have band programs, some of which would likely be in jeopardy without a football program. Certainly the nature of all band programs would change dramatically without football. The biggest part of the band program during the year is participation at football games. Bands provide a special atmosphere at the game by playing upbeat music from the stands; and they march and provide special entertainment for the crowd at halftime. Without football as the centerpiece, the band program would be hard pressed to attract students. After all, band students are almost always graduates of high schools in the state where they were a part of the marching

band which played at football games. Their experience has mostly been gained through playing at football games.

The Mississippi Association of Community & Junior Colleges (MACJC) determines policy for athletics in all sports, including football. Those policies govern all sports within the guidelines set forth the by the National Junior College Athletic Association (NJCAA). The fifteen community college presidents meet each month to consider business of the MACJC. In years past the subject of athletics many times would dominate discussion, even to the extent that other items on the agenda sometimes didn't get the attention they deserved. Athletics was obviously an important item of business, but it was also an item where rarely did everyone agree, since the college programs were extremely competitive. Through the years some have seen the amount of time spent on athletic issues as a "negative" because it tended to take away from other discussion time; however, the fact that sports is such a big part of the community college culture more than justifies a significant amount of time on the agenda for the governing authority. Nevertheless, the MACJA now has a policy in place where the Association will hold a special meeting once per year to discuss athletic matters. A two-thirds majority vote is required to place an athletic matter on the table for discussion at any other meeting during the year.

Mississippi now has its own bowl game for the football champion in Mississippi to play the best team that can be mustered from another state. Mississippi Gulf Coast Community College hosts that bowl game on the gulf coast.

At one time Mississippi had fourteen of the forty-five community college

football teams in the nation. I don't know how that number stands today, but one thing is for certain, Mississippi has more than its share of football teams. What does that mean? It means that football is an integral part of the culture of the Mississippi community college. To put it in a nutshell, football fans who attend Mississippi community college football enjoy the best football that can be found in local communities around the state.

Thanks to Mike Frascogna and his sons for highlighting Mississippi community college football in this book. The facts and stories about Juco football in Mississippi are very special to all of those who have played and coached in the game of football at the two-year college level.

Dr. Howell C. Garner
Executive Director
Mississippi Community College Foundation

ACKNOWLEDGEMENTS

///

There are many people to thank. First and foremost a heartfelt thank you to all those folks who were gracious enough to allow us to interview them for this book. Their help and cooperation was vital to the project.

We are particularly indebted to a number of people at each of the schools in the Mississippi Juco league who provided us with their expertise in reviewing our manuscript. A special thank you to them for sharing their vast knowledge about their respective schools. Those special folks are:

Jones County Junior College: Rebecca Patrick, Dr. Jesse Smith, Katie Herrington and Shawn Wansley.

Hinds Community College: Brian Emory, Ben Fatherree and Robert Smith.

East Central Community College: Bubby Johnston.

East Mississippi Community College: David Rosinski and Nick Clark.

Pearl River Community College: Mitch Deaver and Chuck Abadie

Northwest Mississippi Community College: Kevin Maloney and Bobby Ray Franklin.

Itawamba Community College: Will Kollmeyer and Mike Eaton.

Southwest Mississippi Community College: Michael Gunnell.

Northeast Mississippi Community College: M. Joseph Miller, Tony Finch, Michael H. Miller, Ricky G. Ford, Billy Ward and Ricky Smither.

Mississippi Gulf Coast Community College: Bill Snyder and Ladd Taylor.
Mississippi Delta Community College: Joe Wilson.
Coahoma Community College: Freeman Horton.
Holmes Community College: Steve Diffey.
Copiah-Lincoln Community College: Natalie Davis.
Meridian Community College: Robby Atkinson.

A salute and a nod of appreciation to the outstanding leaders of Mississippi's Community Colleges: Dr. Johnny Allen, Dr. Larry Bailey, Dr. Steven Bishop, Dr. Glen Boyce, Dr. David Cole, Dr. Scott Elliott, Dr. Mary S. Graham, Dr. William Lewis, Dr. Clyde Muse, Dr. Ronnie Nettles, Dr. Vivian Presley, Dr. Jesse Smith, Dr. Gary Spears, Dr. Phil Sutphin and Dr. Rick Young. Also recent retirees, Dr. Willis Lott and Dr. Oliver Young.

For various contributions we would also like to say thank you to John S. Watson for providing us with several of the vintage game programs, Robert Smith and Brian Emory for providing the game photographs for the Hinds chapter, Mitch Deaver for the Pearl River photographs, Stadium Wrap for the player photographs in the recruiting district section of each chapter along with Wilford Case, Paul Benton, Marshall Ramsey, Dr. Howell Garner, Dr. Eric Clark, Charles Russell, Constance Rawlins, Mike Frazier, Steven DeVivo, Greg Pevey, Shawnassey Howell, Janice Virden and Kamel King for their valuable contributions.

The most valuable player on the Juco project was Judy Frascogna, who helped all of us in numerous ways to bring this project to completion.

X.M. Frascogna, Jr.
X.M. Frascogna, III
Martin Frank Frascogna

ABOUT THE CARTOONIST

Marshall Ramsey is the part-time editorial cartoonist for the *Clarion-Ledger* and is nationally syndicated by Creators Syndicate. Ramsey is a two-time Pulitzer Finalist and his cartoons appear in over 400 newspapers nationwide. He also has illustrated seven books by financial expert Dave Ramsey and by chef and author Robert St. John. Ramsey also has had two books of his works published. Ramsey can be heard in the afternoon on The Marshall Ramsey Show on the SuperTalk Mississippi radio network. Ramsey is also a melanoma survivor who has been honored for his work promoting skin cancer screening.

Ramsey and his wife, Amy, and three sons live in Mississippi, the greatest state for junior college football and raising a family.